HUMAN HABITAT:

HOW DO YOU WANT TO LIVE?

HOW DO YOU WANT TO LIVE?

Chairman of the Working Party

THE COUNTESS OF DARTMOUTH *Greater London Councillor*

Members

ROBERT JACKSON *Fellow of All Souls College, Oxford*

SIMON JENKINS *Columnist, London Evening Standard*

PROFESSOR RONALD NICOLL *Chair of Urban and Regional Planning University of Strathclyde*

MRS MICHAEL REYNOLDS *Housewife*

ALFRED WOOD *County Planning Officer, Worcester (Formerly City Planning Officer, Norwich)*

Special Advisers

SIR OVE ARUP, MICE

LORD CLARK, CH KCB FBA

MAX NICHOLSON, CB

Secretariat

KENNETH EVANS

STEPHEN TAYLOR

KATHERINE RENNIE

How do you want to live?

A Report on the human Habitat

Presented in January 1972 to

THE SECRETARY OF STATE FOR THE ENVIRONMENT
THE RIGHT HONOURABLE PETER WALKER MBE MP

*A study of public opinion, undertaken at his request
in connection with the United Nations Conference on the Human
Environment, Stockholm, June 1972*

LONDON HER MAJESTY'S STATIONERY OFFICE 1972

Published for the Department of the Environment

SBN 11 750514 5

Foreword by the Secretary of State for the Environment

This is a report by one of four working parties which I set up last year in preparation for the United Nations Conference on the Human Environment in Stockholm next June. I asked them to contribute to the briefing of the United Kingdom delegation to the Conference, which I shall lead, by collecting and assessing the views of voluntary and private bodies and individuals on the matters the Conference is to discuss.

This and the other reports will be of the greatest value to the delegation and will fortify our ability to contribute to a successful outcome of the Conference. I am arranging for a synopsis of them to be circulated there. Afterwards they will be of help to the Government in developing our policies and proposals in the environmental field. They are clearly the fruit of much imaginative and painstaking work, and I am very grateful to the working parties and to all those on whose contributions the reports are founded.

PETER WALKER

pp. ii, iii: Glantees Farm, Newton-on-the-Moor.

pp. x, xi: Imperial Chemical Industries, Wilton Works, Teesside.

p. 2:   *The Thames at Strand-on-the-Green.*

p. 16:   *Little Moreton Hall, near Congleton, Cheshire.*

p. 36:   *Infill Housing at the Old Town, Corby, Northamptonshire.*

p. 62:   *Eighteenth Century Rum Warehouse, Deptford.*
Turned into flats by the Greater London Council.

p. 98:   *Oak Lane Bridge, Sevenoaks By-Pass A21. Civic Trust Award 1968.*

p. 118:   *Paddington Maintenance Depot, Greater London Council.*
Civic Trust Award 1970.

p. 140:   *Whitworth Art Gallery, University of Manchester.*

p. 168:   *A back garden in Stratford Grove, Putney.*

Edinburgh University Library
Main Library
Receipt of books issued

Today's date:
07/05/2005
01:58 pm

Item How do you want to live? : a report on
the human habitat / Chairman of the

working party: The Countess of Dartmouth.
Date format: yyyy/mm/dd
DUE DATE:2005-06-04 23:59:00

Please return your books
TO THE LIBRARY YOU BORROWED
THEM FROM

MAIN LIBRARY SERVICE CHANGES
From 6 Jan Mon-Thur after 7 pm

and Sats 9-12 during term
Services include: study space,
PCs, self issue only, e-enquiries

*

Contents

		Page
Cover Photograph	SNOWDON	
Drawings	ROY WORSKETT	
Prologue	PHILIP LARKIN	
1 Our Habitat		1
2 People and Planning		15
3 Housing and Architecture		35
4 Conservation Areas and Historic Buildings		61
5 Traffic		97
6 Industry and Commerce		117
7 Recreation		139
8 Environmental Education		167
Epilogue	MAX NICHOLSON	
Summary of Recommendations		187
List of Contributors		193
Acknowledgments for the Photographs		197
Visits		199
Thanks		200
Bibliography		203
Index		207

To The Rt Hon Peter Walker MBE MP
  Secretary of State for the Environment

Dear Secretary of State

We have been considering a vast subject. Our studies have been based on the complaints and views of people who wrote to us either as individuals or representing hundreds of thousands of others in their particular organisations. We have made many visits to different parts of Great Britain. We have read a large number of books and reports on different aspects of the environment. Between us we have written every word of the text of this Report, and unanimously agree the findings.

We hope that you sir, will accept and implement some of our recommendations. We also hope that all those who read it may learn from the past failures or achievements of those in authority, how to balance beauty, humanity and prosperity in the rapidly changing habitat of the future.

Yours sincerely

RAINE DARTMOUTH
Chairman

ROBERT JACKSON

SIMON JENKINS

RONALD NICOLL

ANGELA REYNOLDS

ALFRED WOOD

Prologue

I thought it would last my time—
The sense that, beyond the town,
There would always be fields and farms
Where sports from the village could climb
Such trees as were not cut down;
I knew there'd be false alarms

In the papers about old streets
And split-level shopping, but some
Have always been left so far;
And when the old part retreats
As the bleak high-risers come
We can always escape in the car.

Things are tougher than we are, just
As earth will always respond
However we mess it about;
Chuck filth in the sea, if you must:
The tides will be clean beyond.
—But what do I feel now? Doubt?

Or age, simply? The crowd
Is young in the M1 cafe;
Their kids are screaming for more—
More houses, more parking allowed,
More caravan sites, more pay.
The pylons are walking; the shore,

When you try to get near the sea
In summer . . .
                    It seems, just now,
To be happening so very fast;
Despite all the land left free,
For the first time I feel somehow
That it isn't going to last,

That before I snuff it, the whole
Boiling will be bricked in
Except for the tourist parts—
First slum of Europe, a role
It won't be so hard to win,
With a cast of crooks and tarts.

And that will be England gone,
The shadows, the meadows, the lanes,
The guildhalls, the carved choirs.
There'll be books; it will linger on
In galleries; but all that remains
For us will be concrete and tyres.

Most things are never meant.
This won't be, most likely: but greeds
And garbage are too thickly strewn
To be swept up now, or invent
Excuses that make them all needs.
I just think it will happen, soon.

PHILIP LARKIN

1 Our Habitat

Contents

Public Opinion   3

Working Party
Opinion   9

1   Public Opinion

1.1   **H R H The Duke of Edinburgh** Extract from '*Industrial Management*' 1971
'*In the long run, I believe that this business of the environment is the only, the vital, moral problem of today.*'

1.2   **Mrs T A Thompson** Plymouth
'*I think our habitat has the greatest effect on our lives, for most of us it is our little world, and whatever happens to it, or in it, involves us more than, say, a man flying to the moon.*'

1.3   **Sir Ove Arup**
'*We have reached a stage in the development of our technology where we have the power to create the environment we need or to destroy it beyond repair, according to the use we make of our power. This forces us to control this power. To do this, we must first of all decide what we want to achieve. And this is far from easy and may not be possible at all.*'

1.4   **Imperial Chemical Industries**
'*There is a balance to be struck between what a man, a community, or even a nation, would like to do and what it can afford to do, and this varies in time depending on how rich or poor it happens to be in the period under consideration. When a man is hungry and out of work environment factors are of less importance than his prime needs, and when he is well fed, housed and comfortable the environment in which he lives assumes great importance.*'

1.5   **Emrys Jones** Extract from '**Man and His Habitat**'
'*The major problem is how to accommodate change without destroying the structure of society. Change is constant, however, gradual, however much resisted, in the simplest and in the most complex society. Militating against change is a universal feeling of reluctance to upset an existing way of life. To accommodate change some part of the existing pattern must go, and yet the entire structure must not be damaged. The familiarity of the pattern of everyday existence which spells out the relationships between society and the environment on the one hand and between various members of the society on the other is a strong shelter from the unknown. Against this comforting stability, society faces innovations from within and without which at once threaten and promise, and it is not surprising that many of those who look at the stars and dream of utopias are regarded with suspicion. To many people "planning" is a bad word, not only because it suggests a measure of control and loss of personal freedom, but because it also threatens an established and*

accepted pattern of life. Yet in one sense planning means dealing with change, making more orderly a natural sequence of events, shaping them, perhaps hastening them, but not destroying the past in the process. Indeed, planning should ease the process of accommodating change.'

1.6   **Peter Mason** Consulting Engineer
'It would be relatively straightforward to computer design a habitat for a completely computered society. But man, being fortunately still of spirit as well as flesh, needs a leavening of the natural and unregimented, even if not very cost effective; he needs the security, somewhere, of the old established, even if not particularly efficient or beautiful. This means, inevitably, that the new environment must be developed to march hand in hand with the existing rather than be allowed to sweep it away as of no account.'

1.7   **National Union of Townswomen's Guilds**
'Unless we do something about our habitat now the quality of life is at stake. Minimum noise, conservation of natural beauty, a well preserved environment and good buildings and road systems with everyone sharing in the advantages of modern science and technology—these should be our aims.'

1.8   **Borough Planning Officer** Hounslow
'People are insecure, worried, frustrated, and this reveals itself in a tendency to turn ones back on the world and live in a 'pleasant environment'. It is the result of world conditions, a desire to creep into a cave, an ostrich-like attempt to put one's head under ground.'

1.9   **The Joint Committee** Society for The Protection of Ancient Buildings. Georgian Group—Victorian Society
'Habitat is one of the factors that vitally affects our lives, although often ⸱ ᵒconsciously. It is not the less important because others, such as fear, want, ᵢ. ᵉer, employment are more obvious. In practical terms the successful human habitat, where people are healthy, happy and fulfilled, is difficult to achieve by the theoretical standards laid down by sociologists and planners alone.'

1.10   **The Royal Institution of Chartered Surveyors**
'The recent Government decision on the third London Airport provides a powerful example to illustrate how an exhaustive expert analysis and conclusion was overpowered by a value judgement whose correctness it would be impossible for mathematics to prove.'

1.11   **Hugh Roberts** Tenterden Kent
'A sympathetic environment is an individual matter. It is remarkable how many artists, eg painters can live happily in conditions of squalor. Beauty is not of course the same as prettiness, and most people do not care consciously

4

about their surroundings beyond the limits of their own gardens. The devoted suburban gardener can tolerate total urban squalor.'

1.12   **Wanstead Residents Society**
        'Human beings seem to have the power to survive amongst even the most grim surroundings, but obviously a depressing, ugly, and impersonal environment must seriously reduce the degree of pride that they take in the area in which they live. And if they do not take a pride in their own area, they will not show much consideration towards other areas that they visit, whether through insensitivity or unconscious resentment.'

1.13   **National Union of Journalists**
        'Effective control over the environment in its amenity and aesthetic aspects depends ultimately on the level of awareness of the ordinary citizen. If he ceases to be sensitive to adverse changes in his living environment, however caused, and takes shelter in an introverted domesticity, then he will no longer be concerned to defend the quality of community life.'

1.14   **Royal Society for the Prevention of Accidents**
        'The cause of accidents and the reasons which lie behind them are often deep and involved. We know that the battery hen can suffer severe stress which is due to her environmental conditions and the mismanagement of them. For much the same reason perhaps human beings may suffer accidents or illness.'

1.15   **The Institution of Civil Engineers**
        'The Civil Engineer can suggest schemes for land reclamation, for economy in land use, for improving land to make it suitable for other purposes, or for extending the human habitat into the sea or underground, but he could not presume to give expert opinion on the psychological effects on people of living or working underground or in tall buildings.'

1.16   **Calder Civic Trust** Yorkshire
        'Lack of population control must be paid for by increased "people control".'

1.17   **Plymouth Humanist Group** Devon
        'No-one has suggested that reproduction should be state-controlled. But we should make it acceptable to have two, one or no children. Obviously to foster these attitudes we must make it not only possible but easy for people of all ages to obtain contraceptive advice, sterilization and early abortion. It must be thought of as respectable to resort to these measures.'

1.18   **M H Highfield** Peterborough
        'Our habitats should change and develop slowly and meaningfully; the all-embracing development or development plan, although fashionable and apparently expedient, is an insensitive and damaging instrument, and has not succeeded in producing satisfactory environments.'

1.19   **Sir Paul Reilly** Council of Industrial Design
'There is in all city dwellers a built-in requirement for the three H's—
higgledy-piggledy, huggermugger and hullabaloo. Anyone walking round the
new city centre of Plymouth at nine o'clock at night will appreciate the
gloomy absence of these qualities.'

1.20   **The British Tourist Authority**
'We can see great dangers for the tourist trade, Britain's fourth and most
important export industry, if the structure of our habitat should change, and
if we should lose the historic and cultural features which are a traditional part
of British life, and which are the very reasons that so many seek our shores.'

1.21   **'Tomorrow's London' Greater London Council**—Extract
'One of the features that many Londoners prize so much about their city is the
fact that in between the vast featureless masses of inter-war housing
developments there are still villages, dating back to the middle ages, which
have preserved much of their atmosphere if few of the original structures.
Alternating with the great public buildings of the city centre are small, quiet
enclaves, not necessarily chic town houses, but unpretentious artisan
dwellings, grouped round the local shop, a church, an old school. Some of this
will have to go, because even if we could afford to bring it up to modern
standards, not enough people wish to live under the relatively cramped
conditions which remain even after the plumbing has been improved. In other
'villages' we shall try to preserve much of their character.'

1.22   **Civic Trust for Wales**
'Our habitat has an enormous effect on our lives, but it is difficult to establish
the precise role of the physical compared with the social environment in
assessing the influence of 'place'. For example, a recent study of juvenile
delinquency in Cardiff suggests that adolescents in old and fairly crowded
working class districts have a lower than average record of delinquency,
though when similar families grow up in and are moved to new housing estates,
the incidence of law breaking increases to exceed the average for the city.
While the physical environment of the old areas appears to be sub-standard,
the community spirit, the self-policing attitudes of close-knit family groups,
the presence of social contacts and facilities which have developed over the
years, make them apparently enjoyable to live in; compared with the higher
physical standards, ostensibly better planning, but social sterility of new
estates.'

1.23   **Royal Society for the Protection of Birds**
'It is clear that people get enjoyment and refreshment from contact with
nature. This contact may not be at a sophisticated level, nor need it involve
total quietness and solitude—indeed one would guess that for many people
these are in fact not desired, and hence they sit by their cars in other people's

company to enjoy a view of grass and trees rather than concrete and chimneys. If, then, people require this very simple contact with nature in their lives, it should be provided as a part of their living habitat.'

1.24   Keep Britain Tidy Group

'Litter is not packaging. Litter is people.'

1 Working Party Opinion

1.25 'It's handy for the shops', said the old lady: 'And there's a bit of a garden to sit in on a fine day. I can see the school from here. I like to see children about, but not too close, they can be a bit rough with their games. My younger sister lives near; she moved away once, but she came back. No friends, you see, in the other place. Bingo of course, but the buses weren't good, and nothing for the boys to do in the evening. It was a nice flat, I grant you, but all those big blocks. You couldn't find your way about, and no-one seemed to care.'

1.26 Above all, the habitat must be human. How can this be achieved, or does it just happen? We have examined the problems of major city centres, suburbs, villages, country market towns, and areas suffering from the pressures of either expansion or decline. When we began our studies, we soon realised the interlocking nature of every aspect, just as in The House That Jack Built.

1.27 Consider for a moment neither a major city nor a village, but an imaginary medium-sized town called Barfordbridge. Heavy lorries thundered through and continually polluted the air with noise and fumes. It did not seem worthwhile to clean or repaint houses and shops, and when residents sat in the grubby municipal gardens, they were encircled by traffic. Slowly people began to avoid the High Street. Shopkeepers suffered loss of trade; those who lived in the upper part of old houses in the centre of the town moved away, and the whole area became shabby and neglected. The rateable values went down, and there was a planning application for an out-of-town shopping centre. The Council made efforts to attract new industry, but industrialists took one look and shook their heads. 'We are so sorry', they excused themselves, 'We have to think of our managers and their wives'. The young executives in existing industries answered advertisements for jobs further afield, with their eyes on the new houses going up on former Green Belt land several miles away. The old people stayed in Barfordbridge. They had no choice. They would soon die, just like the town.

1.28 Yet judicious planning could have saved Barfordbridge; just as in Haddington, East Lothian, where determined efforts by the local authorities to attract more industry and new people has rejuvenated the entire town; careful infilling of new housing and a complete facelift for the many historic buildings has made it one of the most attractive places in

opposite: Eardisland, Herefordshire.
pp. 10, 11: Preston Oatmeal Mill, East Linton, Scotland.

Scotland. Deliberate planning policies have also brought people back to live in Cirencester, Gloucestershire, and the housing, both public and private, is brilliantly sited to enhance the environment.

1.29 But expansion can bring other problems in its train. Major industrial cities often have special difficulties with slum clearance, which can result in the breakdown of communities. In new housing developments the initial lack of both social facilities and landscaping can leave unseen and visible scars on the human habitat. New road networks, however necessary, can cause further disruption, and the general upheaval nearly always leads to pressure upon the local authority to release Green Belt land on the outskirts of a city for more building.

1.30 In smaller towns, expansion can destroy the established character and charm, when supermarkets, petrol stations or office blocks of inappropriate scale replace existing historic buildings, and road widening schemes cut off corners and encourage traffic. Yet our towns and cities must be prosperous to survive. All these problems and contradictions can only be resolved by planners and elected representatives who have sensitivity, courage, vision and common sense. The secret is to look at the situation as a whole, since the whole is composed of so many different facets.

1.31 Planning, Housing, Architecture, Traffic, Historic Buildings, Industry, Commerce and Recreation; all of these form part of our habitat, which in turn, influences our behaviour and our attitude to life. Historians may point to artists or musicians whose talents blossomed in a habitat which the majority would find distasteful or degrading, or to rulers and politicians whose ambitions stemmed from a desire to escape from a mean street or an over-crowded home. Not only fame is the spur. Many a millionaire has been determined to leave behind him the squalor of his early surroundings, and there are few parents who do not wish their children to better themselves and to have a more comfortable life. How can we reconcile these very laudable ambitions with an increasing population, a small island, and an economy mainly dependant upon successful manufacturing industries which by their very size and essential requirements hardly enhance the environment?

1.32 We do not share the views of the prophets of doom who point to the lesson of the Gadarene Swine, and who try to make us feel guilty every time we eat or procreate. We hope that the wild guess-work on population growth will be somewhat damped down by the latest figures revealed in 'Long Term Population Trends for Great Britain', recently published by the Department of the Environment. By the year 2001 there may be ten million extra people, an increase of 18%. This is a substantial increase. However, the vagaries of human behaviour have confounded many experts in the past, and in population estimates they provide a built-in factor of uncertainty. But any trend which will put increased pressure upon the facilities and services which are a vital part of our habitat is a serious cause for concern. We await with interest the results of studies now in progress by the Population Panel, set up by the Government in late 1971.

1.33 However fluctuating the estimated figure, where would any extra people actually go? We question the wisdom of allowing five million to settle in the South East, as provided for in the Strategy Plan for that area. It is always possible to cram any amount of people into a given acreage, but does this work in terms of a successful human habitat?

1.34 Land could present an almost insoluble problem. Today, 8% of our land is urbanised. Another 3% will be needed for building by the end of the century. This is an increase of 37%. We continually emphasise throughout the Report that we must resist attempts to build on virgin land unless as a last resort, when there is so much surplus railway land, former dockland, worked-out colliery land, and any other smaller pockets of land which it is possible to reclaim. This should be a fundamental policy, if we are to keep the countryside both for the increasing demands for recreation, and for the industry of agriculture.

The Sea Front at Eastbourne, Sussex.

1.35   The specific emphasis today must be to protect and enhance our existing environment, whilst providing new opportunities for work, new homes and more outlets for leisure. Yet we must not embalm our cities, towns and villages as set pieces for tourists. We must give them new life, decorate them with trees, flowers and greenery, and ensure that modern buildings blend with old to create a habitat which is aesthetic, and financially viable. We do not accept that the two are incompatible.

1.36   Greater care must be taken in the siting of new industries, particularly those which need water, and therefore congregate beside rivers or coast-lines. In many cases industry could make a greater contribution to the environment than at present, but we must avoid imposing restrictions or conditions on industry or commerce which could price our products out of world markets. Jobs are always at stake, and those who preach against economic growth are seldom prepared to lower their own standard of living. Surely we can keep an intelligent balance between conflicting factors?

1.37   In former years, the environment has not been a dominant subject in people's minds. Today it is. We all have higher standards. We want more worldly goods and more attractive surroundings. We also want repose. We want to escape from everyday worries and have fun, but not to sit in a traffic jam for hours on the way to the coast. We want better education for our children and job opportunities when they leave school or university. We want to provide for the future, live in the present, and keep some reminders of the past. We want roots, we want security, we want to belong. We want to live in a habitat which is convenient, which is human, yet containing elements of beauty which can inspire us and lift our spirit towards ambition and adventure. It is the enterprise and ingenuity of her people which has made Britain great. Now is the moment for us to give our time, our talents, and our individual expertise to help achieve an environment which we can all share, can all enjoy, and of which we can all be proud.

2 People and Planning

COUNTY
HALL

Contents

Public Opinion   17

Working Party Opinion   23

Introduction   23

Public Participation   26

Planning Education   30

Compensation   31

Conclusion   31

Recommendations   34

2 Public Opinion

2.1 **Professor Reyner Banham** Extract from **'Los Angeles'**
'The failure-rate of town planning is so high throughout the world that one can only marvel that the profession has not long since given up trying; the history of the art of planning is a giant waste-bin of sumptuously forgotten paper projects.'

2.2 **Professor D R Denman** Cambridge University Department of Land Economy
'We in Britain have among the nations been the pioneers in framing laws to commit into the hands of public authorities powers to plan the use of the physical environment, and we have lessons to teach as a consequence.'

2.3 **Lord Llewelyn Davies and Peter Cowan** University College London Extract from **'Science and the City'**
'The British have a very special attitude towards their countryside and landscape. They like it tamed but romantic and they care greatly that the countryside should be designed. The town planning movement in Britain had its roots in a reaction against urban growth, as represented by the nineteenth century industrial city. Above all the British have felt that the city must be contained—it cannot be allowed to spread across the face of the nation, eating up land unchecked.'

2.4 **Council for the Protection of Rural England—Head Office**
'It should be one of the primary purposes of town and country planning to maintain a sharp physical distinction between town and country. The attainment of high environmental standards is equally important in both, but they have their different characteristics and both are improverished if the distinction between them is blurred.'

2.5 **Professor Asa Briggs** Extract from his paper **'The Sense of Place'** 1967
'When London grows, the plain quantitative question is put: "How can we get land for our surplus population?" And planners often answer it by riding roughshod over local issues associated with "place". Much that is distinctive in individual buildings, and, more important, in whole milieux, has been destroyed not only through the pressure of market forces but through public action. Thus, in Britain, for example, the historic city of Worcester has been massacred since 1945 with acres of medieval streets near the cathedral razed. Where the sense of place has survived, it has been for deliberate reasons of history or for historical reasons which are concealed from view. Warsaw was

rebuilt as it had been after 1945—a triumph of historical feeling not only for place but for the particular visual forms associated with that place—because its rebuilding was a magnificent gesture of pride and hope. Other smaller "places" in the world which have retained their visual identity in the twentieth century and are now treasured for their distinctiveness are places like my own town of Lewes, which escaped some of the nineteenth century social processes. They escaped because they were "off the map'."

2.6 **Professor Colin Buchanan** Extract from **'The Commission on the Third London Airport'**
'There has been a desperate holding action fought against the destructive powers of a population emerging from a state of poverty and urban confinement but as yet unendowed (no fault of theirs) with the standards and principles required for the safe-guarding of a rural environment as fragile as it is valuable. Nevertheless, the effort on the whole has been successfully maintained in the face of the forces of erosion powerfully arrayed. One shudders to think what the face of Britain would now be like had it not been for this sustained effort.'

2.7 **The Knutsford Society** Cheshire
'It is vital for the happiness of most people that they should feel that they belong to a recognisable community, to which they can contribute something of value and which consequently affords them some respect as individuals. It is here that town planning has acquired a bad name by riding roughshod over the social needs of people.'

2.8 **The Crofters Commission** Inverness
'More important even than the habitat is the self respect and the sense of personal independence which is so often lost in an urban environment where the private individual is remote from all the centres of power whether in his work or in the community. It seems to us that planning without consultation and to a certain extent participation by the ordinary citizen is self-defeating and cannot achieve its own aims.'

2.9 **Gordon McLeish** London WC2
'Once people become creatively involved in their own environment it can evolve and improve. The tragedy is that much town planning idealistically conceived fails because planners strive to contain people in a prepared pattern, whereas people are happiest when they are involved adding something of themselves to the communal scene.'

2.10 **R E Pahl** Extract from **'Whose City'**
'Planners are expected to make our life "better", but if they succeed they may be resented—because people are thereby being deprived of the freedom to

plan their lives for themselves. Not only are planners coming increasingly under attack through the mass media at the national level, but they may feel threatened and insecure at the local level as their professional isolation is invaded by public participation. There may thus be a retreat to defending bureaucratic procedures at the very time that a more outward-looking concern with social processes and social problems, is needed.'

2.11   London Borough of Hillingdon
'The commercial considerations of development have predominated in the past and the planning "balance sheet" is still a relative innovation. It is so new that it is apparently capable of misinterpretation by such an august body as the Roskill Commission who were unable to quantify the intangible qualities appertaining to the environment, so they left them out. It was left to the only planner on the Commission to denounce the choice of Cublington as "an environmental disaster".'

2.12   The Westminster Society London
'Much attention needs to be given to the social problems related to the redevelopment of city centres, and to the difficulties of maintaining a balanced residential population where, as in central London, the pressure on land arising from the competing claims of housing, hotels, offices, shops and other places of business, education, entertainments and public institutions inflate land values. Residential redevelopment resulting in increased rents may put the accommodation beyond the means of the lower and middle income groups which are essential to a balanced community.'

2.13   High Wycombe Society Bucks
'One cannot zone a steel rolling mill in the middle of a domestic housing area, but it is wrong to be too clinical in separating the various activities of a community. It tends to create an evening and weekend man, a work man, a shopping man and a recreational man; whereas at one time a community of whole men provided the necessary contact for complete social identity.'

2.14   Brockham Green Village Society Surrey
'The right balance of land use—such decisions should be made by qualified experts, not well-meaning committees of slightly informed laymen.'

2.15   Calder Civic Trust Yorkshire
'Public Authorities too must be persuaded to exercise more care. They complain when vandals break young trees, yet frequently butcher their own in the name of pruning. Vandals may destroy public furniture, whilst Councils break up whole houses and banish the residents to sterile outskirts or high-rise horror.'

2.16 **Reyner Banham, Paul Barker, Peter Hall, Cedric Price** Extract from '**Non-Plan, An Experiment in Freedom**' Published in New Society, March 1969

'The whole concept of planning—the town-and-country kind at least—has gone cockeyed. What we have today represents a whole accumulation of good intentions. Planning is the only branch of knowledge purporting to be some kind of science, which regards a plan as being fulfilled when it is merely completed: there's seldom any sort of check on whether the plan actually does what it was meant to do, and whether, if it does something different, this is for the better or for the worse.

The result is that planning tends to lurch from one fashion to another, with sudden revulsions setting in after equally sudden acceptances. One good recent example, of course, was the fashion for high flats—which had been dying for some time before Ronan Point gave it a tombstone.'

2.17 **B P Moore, Area Planning Officer County Borough of Sheffield** Extract from '**Environmental Improvement and Urban Renewal**'

'People generally are reluctant to leave an area where they have spent the greater part, if not all, of their lives, and where ties of family and friendship are very strong. Such links take on an even more important role as old age approaches. Owner occupiers particularly object to redevelopment. More and more people are now able to speak for themselves and those that cannot have a champion in the local newspaper.'

2.18 **Christopher Alexander** University of California; Extract from '**A City Is Not A Tree**' winner of Kaufman International Design Award 1965

'Those cities which have arisen more or less spontaneously over many years are "natural cities". Those cities and parts of cities which have been deliberately created by designers and planners are "artificial cities". Siena, Liverpool, Kyoto, Manhattan, are examples of natural cities. Levittown, Chandigarh, and the British New Towns are examples of artificial cities. It is more and more widely recognised today that there is some essential ingredient missing from artificial cities. When compared with ancient cities that have acquired the patina of life, our modern attempts to create cities artificially are, from a human point of view, entirely unsuccessful.'

2.19 **Jane Jacobs** Extract from '**The Death and Life of Great American Cities**'

'Most city diversity is the creation of incredible numbers of different people and different private organizations, with vastly differing ideas and purposes, planning and contriving outside the formal framework of public action. The main responsibility of city planning and design should be to develop—insofar as public policy and action can do so—cities that are congenial places for this great range of unofficial plans, ideas and opportunities to flourish, along with the flourishing of the public enterprises.'

2.20   **The Norwood Society** London SE19
'*We realise only too well that the price of a green and pleasant Norwood is eternal vigilance; and we have many problems. One of our greatest problems is that so many people want to live here that things wrought to make this possible may ruin the environment that draws them here. As the incidence of infill estates increases the time draws nearer when Norwood may become one vast estate of "town houses", without character, without balance, without variety and without hope.*'

2.21   **The Hurley Preservation Society** Berkshire
'*A sub-committee of lady members has undertaken to clear litter daily from the village streets, car park and village greens. Many residents and the shopkeepers have agreed to keep their frontages clean and tidy.*'

2.22   **Hammerson Group of Companies** London
'*Our development in the town centre at Salisbury proved very costly not due to the scale and design of the scheme—but due to the prolonged delay before the necessary planning consents were obtained. From start to finish this scheme was in our pipeline for about ten years, and when one considers that money doubles itself, due to compound interest, in about seven or eight years, it can readily be seen that a project which at one time appears viable, in the final analysis can price itself out of the market, whilst years of wrangling are spent with the planners and conservationists.*'

2.23   **Pershore Civic Society** Worcestershire
'*Planning is the means of conservation, it is also the means of total destruction.*'

2.24   **The Chedworth Society** Gloucestershire
'*We were formed specifically to try and preserve the character and beauty of this place, after some unfortunate planning consents had been given. For success in preventing unfortunate siting of new buildings it is of course the first essential that an amenity society should co-operate with, and understand, the planner's difficulties, as well as bringing its own views very firmly to their notice.*'

2.25   **The Leighton Buzzard and District Preservation Society** Bedfordshire
'*The centres of big cities should be reclaimed before the Green Belt is nibbled at.*'

2.26   **The Joint Committee** Society for Protection of Ancient Buildings—
Georgian Group—Victorian Society
'*The competing demands for land in the countryside, for agriculture and recreation, for semi-urban purposes, such as roads, airports etc, for New Towns and town expansion, present an insoluble problem in an island the*

size of Great Britain. With a growing population, a higher standard of living, greater mobility, and shorter working hours, the attack on the countryside is going to intensify over the next twenty-five years to a pitch when it will be very difficult to save the countryside as we have known it in the past. Yet it will be impossible to stem the rising standards of living and next to impossible to stop the population increasing. The most rigorous rationing of countryside taken for urban and semi-urban uses must be adopted by the Government.'

2.27 **British Railways Board**
'The need to conserve land is of paramount importance. The emphasis today is on releasing, or redeveloping, unproductive railway land. More than 30,000 acres have been sold by the Board since 1964.'

2.28 **Ulster Architectural Heritage Society**
'A farmer whose coastal land is sour and salty may violently resent Authority's refusal to allow him to plant a cash crop of caravans. A village grocer may well feel indignant when he is refused planning permission to build a much needed extension of breeze blocks and corrugated iron. On another level, the retired professional man who lives in a neat pebble-dashed bungalow in a seaside village may well resent paying higher rates to provide facilities for the hordes of summer visitors who spoil the privacy of his street. How far is Government interference with the rights of the individual to go?'

2.29 **Emrys Jones** Extract from **'Man and His Habitat'**
'Successful planning today is that which will enable the next generation to plan successfully. In so far as the past is enshrined in the present, much of this will be handed on to the future: not the trivial and banal, the bric-a-brac of society, but the fundamental and deep-rooted values that are basic to it. In this sense it behoves all planners to be students of the past.'

2 Working Party Opinion

Introduction

2.30 Planners have a bad name. 'They' bulldoze whole areas and drive residents away. 'They' allow huge tower blocks to replace familiar buildings in town centres. 'They' destroy community spirit and drive motorways through historic villages. But before we start the tumbrils rolling, let us consider for a moment why planning came into existence. During the Industrial Revolution hundreds of thousands of people left the countryside and crowded into the cities to find work. They flocked to the iron town of Middlesbrough, to the busy looms of Bradford, to the docks of Liverpool and to the shipyards of Glasgow. Pressure for housing was enormous, and tenements and cellars were rapidly built near the mills or the factories, whose chimneys belched out smoke day and night.

2.31 Professor Sir Colin Buchanan, in The Commission On The Third London Airport, writes: 'Planning was born out of back-to-back houses, out of overcrowding, out of privies in back yards, out of children with nowhere to play, out of ribbon development and urban sprawl, out of countryside despoiled and monuments destroyed. It was born out of painfully gathered experience over a century of industrialism which made it abundantly clear that market forces in land, left to their own devices, fail utterly to produce a humane environment'.

2.32 Can we sit here today, encircled by Green Belts, safe in our residential zones from the threat of a factory in our neighbour's back garden, taking for granted parks in the towns and in the countryside; motorways which facilitate business, commerce and industry upon which our prosperity depends; historic buildings protected by a series of planning acts; and then turn round and berate the planners and the laws which have made it possible to protect our island from uncontrolled building from Lands End to John O'Groats?

2.33 From all parts of the world foreigners come to admire the results of our planning system. They come to see our New Towns, in which nearly three quarters of a million people live at low densities; to visit Peterlee, where on reclaimed mining land houses are built in groups on rafts of reinforced concrete; to visit Stevenage where over 60,000 people live amid trees and greenery in houses whose Radburn layout releases children from fear of traffic, and where paths marked with a special pattern of stones, like Ariadne's thread, lead to the schools and to the neighbourhood shopping centres; to Basingstoke, expanded under the Town Development Act of

1952, where the well laid-out industrial area of manufacturing and servic industries provides over 31,000 jobs; to Coventry, where the pedestria shopping precinct bright with shrubs and flowers, attracts shoppers fro all over the Midlands. Without planning, could all this just have happened

2.34   In Clydebank, Scotland, new housing has been positioned on a hill to giv residents superb views of the mountains beyond the estuary of the Clyd dockside tenements are being demolished, and the land cleared an re-zoned to attract new industry to the area. The entire town centre Thornaby, Teeside, has been newly created several miles inland from i former site, away from the pollution of the factories. In Fife, Scotlan where coal mining used to provide the bulk of the employment, the Coun Council have made massive efforts to attract 130 new industries to th area since 1964, when the opening of the Forth and Tay Road Bridg forged a fast new link with Edinburgh and Dundee. Careful plannin policies in many parts of Great Britain, to create employment, to re-loca industry on new trading estates, or well away from residential district have resulted in considerable improvements including green fingers a environmental areas in many large cities—but there is still a lot to be don

2.35   As far back as 1909, the Housing and Town Planning Act referred to a ne for the introduction of planning into local authority activities. In 1938, t Green Belt, London and Home Counties Act gave specific powers to loc authorities in that area to preserv and acquire open space. Sir Patri Abercrombie, in his imaginative development plans which gained mu from the pioneering work of Sir Patrick Geddes, outlined the plannin principles of both the green belt and the ring road system; and his wor together with that of his contemporaries, culminated in the creation New Towns all over Great Britain. The 1947 Town and Country Plannin Act removed once and for all an owner's right to do as he wished with land, gave powers to reduce housing densities, and for the direction industry to depressed areas. The broad objectives also aimed at t intelligent conservation of our architecture, our countryside and o natural resources. Lord Justice Scott and Sir Montague Barlow we pioneers in the field of countryside planning and relocation of indust Baron Augustus Uthwatt defined the principles of fair compensation compulsory purchase; and the many ideas for the protection of t environment and for the protection of the public interest, resulting in t 1968 and 1969 Acts with their emphasis on strategic policies and structu plans, originated from British town planners whose work has been admir and copied throughout the world. Nevertheless, planners are unpopular the present time. It is essential that we find out what has gone wrong, a whether there is a case to alter and improve our present planning syste

New Offices incorporating Church Tower at Park Circus, Glasgow.
New Housing in Ross's Close, Haddington, East Lothian.

Public Participation

2.36   The idea that the process of planning should be broadened to include the 'planned' has only become widely accepted in the last decade. Previously, the democratic element in the preparation of policies to guide the course of a community's physical and social development was assumed to be provided through the local electoral system. If local councillors and the committees on which they served could not look after the interests of the 'planned', then who could? Alternative channels might not only be arbitrary, but also unconstitutional. These arguments were laid to rest by the Skeffington Report in 1969. An orgy of enthusiasm for 'participation' erupted in every conceivable guise. The growth of amenity societies; heightened interest in community action; increased attention paid to environmental issues by the press; and a number of well-publicised 'causes celebres' such as the London motorway proposals and the third London Airport debate, all thrust the 'planned' to the front of the stage.

2.37   In practice, however, public participation has been rather a damp squib. It is undeniably true that nowadays, specific local planning issues receive much more publicity than a few years ago. Council information officers are ready with handouts and some local authorities even arrange travelling exhibitions in caravans complete with photographs and drawings. But planners still remain suspect, and the public feel that any control over changes to their immediate environment still eludes them. On the whole, consultation has been regarded by local people as an exercise in public relations. Since many planners take the same view, this is not surprising.

2.38   The whole concept of public participation is bedevilled by vagueness and imprecision. The Skeffington Report itself, despite many admirable suggestions, left a multitude of questions unanswered. The result has been some incongruous efforts at participation. There have been local meetings so badly publicised that the speakers outnumbered the audience: there have been plans displayed in town halls located miles away from the areas they affected; there have been questionnaires couched in planner's jargon totally incomprehensible to ordinary people; there have been exhibitions full of highly idealised representations of what may reappear after the threatened demolition has taken place. Most serious of all, there has been a failure to understand that consultation is pointless if it fails to include a clear element of choice. All these failures have caused unnecessary bad blood between planners and the public, and the consequent political upheavals have often delayed the implementation of much-needed improvements.

2.39   The first lesson that has been learned from experiences over the past few years is that people tend to be most concerned when a plan threatens their own street. This may sound selfish, but it is perfectly natural. They are seldom interested in vague overall problems which fascinate planners. One of the clearest features of the consultation on the Greater London Council Development Plan was the insistence on the part of one local group after another to bring planners down to earth to discuss the plans for their own particular area. 'Strategic' planning, as required by the 1968/69 Town and County Planning Acts, has become an intellectual concept requiring its own special language. One result of this has tended to be that strategy is determined without public participation and then a presentation of the consequences, usually without alternatives, is made to local communities. Participation then becomes protest, with the usual pattern of embittered resistance, demonstrations, letters to newspapers, angry meetings, expensive delays and eventual revision of the plans.

2.40 Ad hoc institutions have emerged—from 'Street Defence Leagues' to the more political 'Homes Before Roads' campaign which put up candidates for the 1969 GLC elections. There has been one attempt, however, to organise neighbourhood feeling by holding genuine local elections to a 'Neighbourhood Council'. This is in London, in the Golborne ward of North Kensington. A locally elected council, supported by a foundaton grant, has been in operation for almost a year. It has no official powers, but purports to speak for the neighbourhood. It is doubtful if this pattern is applicable in many parts of the country. It depended heavily on individual enthusiasm, outside support, and most significant of all, on the fact that the area was undergoing rapid and radical change. There may be a lot to fight for in Golborne. There may be considerably less in a Surrey suburb or a West Country village.

2.41 The most successful examples of local participation in planning have been where the authorities have learned to speak the language of local residents, where they have been flexible enough to put forward several alternatives, and where the problems themselves have affected a fairly small area. The fact that a problem may seem small-scale to a planner, does nothing to lessen its importance to the people actually concerned. It is a well-known phenomenon that the most apparently sophisticated and intelligent resident can become obsessively involved in the felling of a single tree, or the siting of a lamp post, if it happens to be in front of his own house. In Clarendon Park, Leicester, where the council were introducing a general improvement area involving considerable changes to the district, they gave extensive publicity to a range of proposals, and the planners sought out 'leaders' among residents in each group of streets who were asked for the views of local people. The result was not only an improved version of the actual proposals but a wider public acceptance of the need for change. In Richmond upon Thames, Surrey, the local amenity society were able to counter the Council's traffic plan for the town with a considerably more sophisticated one of their own.

2.42 One difficulty in trying to involve local people in the planning process is to ensure that the spokesmen are really representative. Unknown activists

often emerge just when the trouble starts and purport to be leading a campaign to save the area from the wicked planners. How do we ensure a balance of local opinion between the joiners and the non-joiners? Whether the silent majority agree or disagree with the vocal minority, there is no doubt that the majority tend to be silent even on the really important matters. One answer is to remember that participation can mean intellectual criticism as well as popular consultation. Many planners have been far more vulnerable to well-directed cross-questioning during a public inquiry from an intelligent outsider than they have to a multitude of local meetings and questionnaires.

2.43 On a wider level, a number of suggestions have been put forward for trying to gauge public reaction to different planning priorities. One of the most ingenious is the 'choice-box' developed by a group called Social and Community Planning Research and tested by Camden Borough Council. It shows the residents a variety of improvements to his environment expressed by a series of pictures. He is given counters symbolising money which he can spend on different improvements. Some are more expensive than others. When the resident has spent all his counters, the planning authority can get some idea of how he would establish priorities between better roads, more parks, improved shopping facilities and so on. Such games can help if only to make planners more aware of public opinion.

2.44 We feel, however, that the most important single element is publicity. It is still extraordinary how many local authorities do not give out to local groups and interested parties full details of planning applications and other proposals affecting an area's future. There should be no excuse for a householder to be obliged to say about a proposal which may intimately affect his way of life: 'I didn't know it was going to happen'. It is not his responsibility to find out. The planners should ensure that he knows.

2.45 We feel it would be most helpful if there could be a specific procedure laid down by the local authority associations, for local publicity of all planning proposals beyond the merely trivial. This procedure should have a name, and all planning authorities should be asked to conform to it. This does not only mean press notices and circulars to immediately interested parties. It should include wide-spread and easily readable publicity material; full briefings to the local press; a regular and free news-sheet to all ratepayers. For large development proposals there should be an exhibition in the neighbourhood. One excellent example of this was the display arranged by the Kensington and Chelsea Borough Council in the central hall of Harrods of hotel proposals for Gloucester Road. The exhibition included models, photographs of the existing site with a photomontage of the hotel superimposed in close-up and from a distance, and a clear questionnaire asking for views.

Bourton-on-the-Water, Gloucestershire.

2.46 It is becoming ridiculous to see planning applications gliding through loca authorities only to be called back for public enquiry after local feeling ha been aroused and an outcry has followed. Apart from anything else, suc a process is exceedingly expensive for taxpayers, ratepayers, architects an developers.

2.47 Even these suggestions do not meet the whole bill. Local people outsid political hierarchies are demanding to be more closely involved in plannin policies. It is a demand that has already been met in the field of education There is no reason why outside representatives should have seats on a education committee while a member of a local amenity society or th chamber of commerce is excluded from the planning committee. We fee that members from such established groups should be co-opted on t planning committees. We also think that the press should be admitted t planning committee meetings. The committees would obviously reserv the right to exclude any non-elected persons when sensitive financia matters are being discussed. It is sometimes said that more open plannin committees would simply result in important decisions being take elsewhere at party political meetings and through chairman's action. Thi can happen already. The presence of informed outsiders could bring mor contentious issues to the surface earlier on, thus perhaps avoiding ope warfare later. It should stimulate more frequent debates on strategi matters and the fact that there may be local opposition to a proposal i less likely to be overlooked than is so often the case today. But if certai councils are reluctant to agree with this proposal—however much lip service they may pay to the virtues of more open planning—we feel ther would be a case for a government direction.

Planning Education

2.48 Another aspect of the growing demand by the public for more knowledg about planning matters, is their uneasy feeling that members of plannin committees are not as well-informed as they should be. We suggest that series of films on different aspects of planning, such as Comprehensiv Redevelopment, Conservation, Re-Location of Industry, New Towns Motorway Design, Environmental Improvements in towns and cities, an so on, should be made by the Department of the Environment in conjunc tion with the Civic Trust, The Town and Country Planning Associatio and other expert bodies, and be made available to every local authorit throughout the country. Lectures should also be arranged, and a members of planning committees should be requested to attend. Councillo are often put on to a planning committee with no expert or even practica knowledge of the subject, and they would find it invaluable to learn c experiences in other towns and cities.

Compensation

2.49 Much of the anxiety over development plans and the inevitable changes they bring about, might be prevented if there were a wider definition of the concept of compensation for loss of property and loss of amenity caused by planning decisions. The Compulsory Purchase Act of 1965 consolidated existing provisions which date back to the Lands Clauses Acts of the last century. These, together with cases decided by the courts, have established that the owner gets a fair market price for his property, plus disturbance. But the law still bears harshly upon some people displaced by local authorities, for example traders and shopkeepers in a small way of business. Hardship may arise because a business tenant can suffer loss of trade over a period of years where a whole district is being redeveloped; the compensation he gets when bought out is diminished for the very reason that his business has become depressed. Small traders running on short tenancies often do not get enough compensation for them to open up in other premises. This kind of hardship could be put right at small cost to the community. There is another point. Compensation is not usually paid without acquisition. At present a freeholder is unable to get a grant for sound-proofing or double-glazing to help him endure a new motorway. Surely this should be changed? The Highways Act of 1959 also makes it necessary to define the land required for a new road. If this could be more generously interpreted, so that an authority could acquire more land than the bare minimum, many engineers have told us they could greatly improve the landscaping and so reduce the visual impact. Even more important, owners of property not actually in the path of the motorway but near enough to be seriously affected, could be bought out with benefit all round. We are not asking for a blank cheque, but a redefinition of the limits at present imposed. First, so that property just outside the line of a new road but seriously affected by it, can be acquired; second, to enable grants to be made to owners for sound-proofing and similar work; third, and this does not only apply to roads, for more flexibility in assessing the compensation payable to owners who, under the present application of the law, seem to be unfairly treated.

Conclusion

2.50 We have considered very carefully whether the current dissatisfaction with planning is due to the inadequacy of the planning laws; but we have come to the conclusion that it is the application of those laws which is at fault. It is perfectly right that there should be powers to effect slum clearance, to organise new road networks or to improve derelict areas. In many cases there has been an appalling lack of sensitivity in their application. There has been a disastrous lack of control over high buildings generally and particularly in historic areas of cities. There has been little understanding of the organic growth of towns, and this has resulted in the eruption of modern buildings in unsuitable places which destroyed established character and street patterns. Most damaging of all, planning permissions have been given for architecture we can only describe as brutal, and which will continue to threaten many towns and cities for years to come. We feel that members and officers of all local authorities should take a long hard look at their own areas, and ask themselves whether the mote is in their own eye.

2.51 Successful planning, just like everything else, depends upon the right people. We have met in our visits round the country, many planning officers whose imagination and drive has created enthusiasm throughout their entire departments for sensitive planning and a policy of improving the environment. We have met councillors who had obviously lost touch with the electorate, and who were simply not interested in the environment. We talked to others who in the most unlikely places were determined to create beauty out of mediocrity, and to those who had spent years in unselfish, unpaid service to the people they represented. The dedication of many council members and officers was often inspiring. But not everyone can have a vision, or the time and energy to make it a reality. If we ourselves are not prepared to make greater individual efforts to protect and improve the area in which we live then we will get the planning we deserve.

opposite: Carshalton Ponds, Sutton, Surrey.
below: The Upper Pedestrian Shopping Precinct, Coventry.

Recommendations

1   *When planning authorities consult interested parties on planning decisions, they should offer alternatives. The financial and environmental consequences must be made clear and the choice should be put before the public in simple language.*

2   *There should be a specific, universal, and named procedure to give local publicity to all planning proposals beyond the merely trivial.*

3   *It should be standard practice for outside representatives to be co-opted on to local planning committees.*

4   *The Press should also be admitted to planning committees; all non-elected persons could be asked to leave when delicate financial matters are being discussed.*

5   *The Department of the Environment, together with the Civic Trust, the Town and Country Planning Association, and other bodies, should make a series of films on different aspects of planning to be shown to local authorities throughout the country.*

6   *The Government should amend the laws relating to compensation:*

    a *so that property just outside the line of a new road, but seriously affected by it, can be acquired.*

    b *To enable grants to be made to owners for sound-proofing and similar work without acquisition.*

    c *To allow more flexibility in assessing compensation payable to small traders who at present suffer hardship due to redevelopment of their area, or due to other planning decisions.*

3 Housing and Architecture

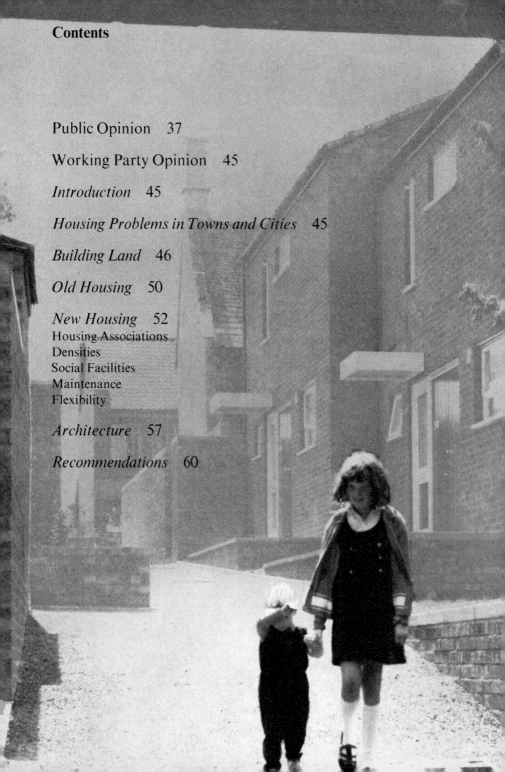

Contents

Public Opinion   37

Working Party Opinion   45

Introduction   45

Housing Problems in Towns and Cities   45

Building Land   46

Old Housing   50

New Housing   52
Housing Associations
Densities
Social Facilities
Maintenance
Flexibility

Architecture   57

Recommendations   60

3 Public Opinion

3.1 **Lord Clark** Extract from **'Civilisation'**
'If I had to say which was telling the truth about Society, a speech by a Minister of Housing or the actual buildings put up in his time, I should believe the buildings.'

3.2 **Trish Hettena** London
'Why is it that so much modern architecture is banal, boring and anachronistic.'

3.3 **Lichfield Civic Society** Staffs
'A good environment should be human in scale. Imposing buildings have a place but none should dwarf human activity.'

3.4 **Council for the Protection of Rural England** Warwickshire Lyndon Cave
'A sympathetic environment is one with which I can cope—which is of a scale I can comprehend. I find vast new roads, especially the new intersections, frighteningly large. I detest supermarkets. I like familiarity—too many new developments and changes make me feel alienated. I like a sense of belonging, of identity and continuity.'

3.5 **Sir William Lithgow and Professor Nicoll** Extract from **'Oceanspan'** 'A maritime-based strategy for European Scotland'
'There is more than ever before, a real need to consider what people want and will enjoy rather than what they will accept. From the past we should have learned that nothing is gained by cutting corners and creating financial prosperity amongst environmental squalor.'

3.6 **London Borough of Barking**
'We have in fact built several tower blocks, but experience, going back for more than ten years, has shown that the "street on end" creates problems of isolation and loneliness which can have severe effects on both adults and children. The psychological problems created by such forms of dwellings have been to a great extent overlooked in town planning and may give rise to serious social problems in the near future.'

3.7 **Dr Hugh Freeman** Manchester
'There is evidence in both Britain and the USA that changing from a closely-knit, traditional working class community to a more open and distant one will affect part of the population adversely. Those affected will be primarily

people who are vulnerable to start with, and who need the support of relatives and familiar surroundings.'

3.8 **Professor D Jones** Bristol University

'Recently our first year students were sent out to look at and compare new flats and so called "slum dwellings". They came back unanimously in favour of the slum dwellings. There you had your bit of garden for your pigeons or for mending your bike. Your van or car stood almost outside the front door and the pavement between was your piece of pavement; the kids could play football down the street, and the scale of it all was human scale. In the flats on the other hand the grass was trim and well-tended but you were not allowed to use it. The access to your flat, which was a row of windows on the umpteenth floor, was by lift. So you never met your neighbours. You didn't really have any anyway. You certainly had a bath and a water closet and I wonder to what extent you had other things that matter?'

3.9 **Anthony Crosland MP** Extract from **'Towards a Labour Housing Policy' 1971**

'There is no unique and objective way of setting a total housing target. We can easily set a minimum figure which will meet our most pressing and urgent needs. But above that minimum the target will depend on a set of personal and social judgements—in particular, over how many years do we seek to replace or improve the existing stock of obsolescent dwellings, and how do we define obsolescence in the future when we take account of these wider environmental factors.'

3.10 **Pershore Civic Society** Worcestershire

'We consider beyond any possible doubt that housing should consist of a mixture of old houses properly repaired and modernised: new houses and moderate sized blocks of low rise flats where these would be suitable. In the past, many old houses have been destroyed which had many useful years of life left in them if suitably repaired and modernised. This has at last been recognised, and excellent grants for both repair and modernisation now exist. We consider a useful idea would be to make a series of short TV films showing this in process. So many people do not yet realise the possibilities of old buildings, nor do they realise what excellent grants are available.'

3.11 **The Islington Society** London

'There is a large demand for old houses and it is these that make up the majority of buildings in a historic environment. Existing grants to owner-occupiers seem adequate, but the Department of the Environment positively discourages rehabilitation by local authorities by giving much larger subsidies for new development. Subsidies for rehabilitation should be at least as much, and in the case of historic areas should be more, than the subsidy for new work.'

3.12   **Desmond Morris** Extract from **'The Human Zoo'**

'The human animal requires a spatial territory in which to live that possesses unique features, surprises, visual oddities, landmarks and architectural idiosyncrasies. Without them it can have little meaning. A neatly symmetrical, geometric pattern may be useful for holding up a roof, or for facilitating the prefabrication of mass-produced housing-units, but when such patterning is applied at the landscape level, it is going against the nature of the human animal. Why else do children prefer to play on rubbish dumps or in derelict buildings, rather than on their immaculate, sterile, geometrically arranged playgrounds?'

3.13   **Hammerson Group of Companies** London

'Many areas of dereliction should be cleared absolutely. In cities such as Leeds, Bradford, Manchester, there have been for years acres and acres of land immediately outside the centres where for one reason or another derelict property has been allowed to stand and present an increasing eyesore. An extension of this is the land which is tantamount to waste land flanking many miles of our railways. Old goods yards, stations and signal boxes just seem to be left to fall into decay.'

3.14   **The Royal Society of Health**

'There should be a wide variety of houses to cater for different types of households; local authorities, and housing in general should consist of a mixture of houses, flats, and modernised old buildings, as well as the provision of special accommodation for old people.'

3.15   **Council for the Protection of Rural England** Devon Branch

'Until the 20th century, individual bungalow development was virtually unknown in Devon. Such alien development is, through sheer numbers, ruining the County, and the bungaloid epidemic is accentuated by the multitude of inappropriate building materials invariably embodied in the construction of the buildings.''

3.16   **William Cowburn** Lancashire

'It might be that public housing as such should be completely abandoned. Instead everyone must be entirely in private housing, with subsidised purchase for lower income groups.'

3.17   **Association of Municipal Corporations**

'The effect of drab, dismal sub-standard housing cannot be overestimated. Squalid surroundings where people live in sub-standard houses alongside sub-standard industrial development of the last century has a permanent effect on the lives of those brought up there, yet on the other hand a community spirit certainly exists in the densely populated but nevertheless intimate terraced streets and the less prosperous housing areas; much of this

community spirit has been destroyed by post-war redevelopment particularly high rise accommodation. One lesson which has been learned is the need for careful programming of clearance work and new building operations to preserve in turn street communities.'

3.18 **National House Builders Registration Council. Director General's personal views**

'Speculative house-builders argue that the right way to promote happiness is to allow the customer to choose what he wants to have within a framework of a minimum planning control. They claim not always reasonably that the worst social disasters have been perpetuated where the rule of, "leave it to the customer", was not observed. They also claim that high rise flats would never have been built in the private sector because they are high in cost but low in customer appeal. The counter-argument by the public sector is that these had to be built in the public sector because of the need of high density. This argument is not, however, wholly convincing. There are many well-meaning people who five years ago advocated high flats as being worthy in their own right, and who did not then sufficiently appreciate that the attitude of British families might be different from that of continental families.'

3.19 **The Royal Institution of Chartered Surveyors**

'The most important element in the human habitat is the dwelling. Too many dwellings in Britain are too small, too old, too obsolete. Those dwellings are mostly occupied by the type of householder least able financially to help himself. There is no incentive for private investors to take a hand in building new dwellings for this most modest kind of tenant, because sixty years of legislation have made it impossible to obtain a remunerative return from investment of that kind. This is a very serious situation, striking at the very root of national development.'

3.20 **Peter Shepherd** Ex-President Royal Institute of British Architects

'Architects vary like doctors and lawyers, some are good—some bad. Unfortunately in architecture, failure shows.'

3.21 **Brian Batsford MP** Extract from lecture to Royal Society of Arts

'The mess of modern Britain, its dreary architecture, its litter, its jumble of street signs and advertisements, is regrettably as much part of our heritage as any historic building or stretch of downland. This is because neither the voices of reason—of Ruskin or Morris or Clough Williams-Ellis or Betjeman or Sandys—nor the initiative of national or local societies—nor the powers of government or local authorities have been strong enough to compete with a steady deterioration in our standards.'

3.22   **Sir Nikolaus Pevsner** Extract from **'Pioneers of Modern Design'**

'The warmth and directness with which ages of craft and a more personal relation between architect and client endowed buildings of the past may have gone for good. The architect, to represent this century of ours, must be colder, cold to keep in command of mechanized production, cold to design for the satisfaction of anonymous clients.'

3.23   **Royal Institute of British Architects**

'It is not generally appreciated that the prime determinants of the built environment are not in any sense architectural. Economic, political, commercial and social factors control most of the major design decisions to such an extent that the actual designer has, all too often, to devote his ingenuity to making the best of a bad job, finding a way to bend the rules to create something which is remotely humane. An obvious example of this is the Housing Cost Yardstick, a bureaucratic cost control tool which has been inflated into the principal determinant in public sector housing. The whole economic and fiscal context in which he works forces the architect to cut initial capital costs at the expense of future cost in use.'

3.24   **D R G Marler** Capital and Counties Property Company Ltd

'I am personally depressed at the generally low architectural and environmental developments which have taken place in this country since the war. I do not accept the view that this is wholly due to penny-pinching property developers. Certainly in this Company we have been prepared to pay the modest increase in building costs which is all that is required.'

3.25   **Stephen Gardiner** 'Observer', architectural correspondent

'Since when did a good idea cost more than a bad one? A much better slogan would be: Good design makes money.'

3.26   **The Civic Trusts Awards 1970** Extract

'Among the major design difficulties today is the problem of coordination: Civic Trust Awards are concerned not only with the architecture of buildings, but with their relationship one to another, their associated surroundings and, above all, with their contribution to the townscape as a whole.

There is a conspicuous lack of effort in this direction, not least among the departments of those very local authorities who are charged with the main responsibility for such coordination. Some otherwise excellent submissions have had to be rejected because landscaping remained hideously incomplete.'

3.27   **Simon Jenkins** Extract from **'A City at Risk'**

'The late sixties saw a popular revulsion against the conventional architectural wisdom of the day that has already had dramatic impact on attitudes to public housing. The tower blocks of flats erected over the past two decades, particularly in areas such as the East End of London, have proved so

inhuman and destructive of neighbourhood relations that people are simply refusing to live in them. A type of accommodation that may be admirably suited to middle-class urban living, where social ties are less geared to geographical proximity, has proved quite unsuited to communities used to the communal intimacy but physical privacy of traditional back-to-back housing People did not like the architecturally exciting products of modern local housing departments. Only now are we at last seeing—in such developments as those at Lillington Street in Pimlico and Reporton Road in Fulham—a new form of low rise high density housing that is proving remarkably successful in human terms. And even in the field of middle-class housing, there can l detected a movement towards revivalism and against originality that is alarming to anyone interested in the health of architectural innovation. Could one not suggest that when the town environment becomes dominated by materials such as glass, concrete and steel, people yearn for more human surroundings when they get home?'

3.28   **London Borough of Islington** K G Blythe—Borough Planning Officer
'With the increasing demands for more space in our homes they should be designed from the outset with future extensions in mind. The current vogue for loft conversions and lounge extensions shows this demand. People would then avoid having to move to find a larger house. Conversely dwellings could have removable rooms so that when families grow up and space demands are reduced a spare bedroom could be removed. This could be particularly applicable to local authority dwellings and would avoid aged parents having to move to smaller dwellings, and lose their community contacts. The initial design of the dwelling could provide for a packaged "lift-off" bedroom above a single storey rear extension, rather in the same way that packaged bathrooms are now being added to dwellings.'

3.29   **Michael Baily** Founder of the Cockaigne Housing Association Ltd Hatfield, Hertfordshire
'An additional stimulus would be something on the lines of a government-backed housing environment trust, able to make grants for environmentally worthwhile projects not readily financed through development funds. This could be backed up by a small technical panel able to recommend developments not conforming to current building and planning regulations; a body enlightened local authorities would welcome.'

3.30   **The Victorian Society**
'The modern planner would do well to study the nineteenth century prototype of the terrace—an architectural form which works, which is adaptable to single housing units or to flats, and which allows a sense of identity and individuality within a fairly tight framework—all of which the tower block fails to achieve.'

3.31 **Evelyn Denington** Chairman, Stevenage Development Corporation
Extract from 'The Contribution of Dispersal' **High Density and Family
Life**

*'Extensive high density building becomes oppressive. There are grave
disadvantages for families with children. Indeed, it is for family life when the
children are young or in early adolescence that high density housing is
particularly wrong.*

*Single people, particularly the young, but also the elderly and middle-aged
can live more happily and easily together in flats at higher densities, although
many of them prefer the more attractive environment produced by lower
densities. If densities are too high they drive out the middle income and
professional people who want owner-occupation. The result is a one-type,
one-class society left in the redevelopment areas to the impoverishment of all
aspects of civic life. There is discontent because those who are left feel
trapped in an environment that they inwardly resent because it is inimical to
the human spirit and totally unsatisfactory for the upbringing of children.
Housing densities in the inner areas of cities must therefore be decreased and
made much more varied. Owner-occupation must be retained in all districts
and lower paid workers must not find themselves closed in extensive ghettos.'*

3.32 **Jane Jacobs** Extract from **'The Death and Life of Great American Cities'**

*'No good for cities or for their design, planning, economics or people, can
come of the emotional assumption that dense city populations are, per se,
undesirable. In my view, they are an asset. The task is to promote the city
life of city people, housed, let us hope, in concentrations both dense enough
and diverse enough to offer them a decent chance at developing city life.'*

3.33 **Le Corbusier**

*'How are we to enrich our creative powers? Not by subscribing to
architectural reviews, but by undertaking voyages of discovery into the
inexhaustible domain of nature! I wish that sometimes architects would take
up their pencils to draw a plant or a leaf, or to express the significance of the
clouds, the ever-changing ebb and flow of waves at play upon the sands.'*

overpage: Backcauseway, Culross, Fife.

3   Working Party Opinion

Introduction

3.34   As our island becomes more crowded, we need a larger stock of higher standard housing, yet there is an increasing disenchantment with the quality of environment which is the result of modern architecture and modern planning methods. It is ironic that much of this dissatisfaction stems from the massive efforts which have been made to cater for housing needs. We are now faced with a number of important questions. Do we spend too little on the roof over our heads? Could the country benefit by improving the quality of its building stock? Are there enough incentives to encourage conservation and improvement of older property? Do our current policies lead to dereliction in town centres? Should positive steps be taken to make town centres and inner areas of large cities more attractive places to live in? Is it too easy to build, and have we enough land for housing without further erosion of the Green Belt?

Housing Problems in Towns and Cities

3.35   Over 80% of Britain's population is concentrated in urban areas. During most of this century, a large movement of people away from town and city centres has taken place, as increased mobility and a higher standard of living have enabled more people to live in suburbia. This exodus has left some town centres to cater exclusively for commerce, and in other places has led to widespread decay. The 1947 Town and Country Planning Act required local authorities to define separate zones for housing, commerce or industry; but nowadays, due to the sharp increase in land prices and building costs, some local authorities feel that mixed land uses are essential if our cities are to survive as balanced organisms. The urban environment must be made more attractive and people need to have within easy reach employment, shops, schools, social facilities and green open space.

3.36   Most towns and cities had, or still have, an inner core of older housing connected to a group of small shops, a pub, a school or perhaps a social club. When the houses became obsolete, they were swept away in a slum clearance programme together with the existing social life, and were replaced by tower blocks which are so much criticised today. Cities such as Glasgow and Liverpool which in the nineteenth century were under great housing pressure from people who came to work in the rapidly expanding industries of that time, have had to cope in the twentieth century with a vast stock of housing which was rapidly deteriorating all at once. It is impossible to compare the problems of those big industrial areas with smaller towns, where it often seems that in housing redevelopment a sledgehammer has been used to crack a nut.

3.37 The architecture of new local authority housing schemes is often inhuman in scale and the featureless blocks have eroded the individual character of towns and cities so that many look exactly the same. This is partly due to financial restrictions and cost yardsticks imposed by the Government in order to ensure that housing conformed with certain standards. It is also caused by Building Regulations which were introduced to cushion a less-protected people against inferior buildings, bad ventilation, loss of day-light and inadequate drainage but are nowadays often a severe restriction upon the architectural profession. In private housing schemes the limited finances of clients may impose a further restriction on design, and some building societies are reluctant to advance capital for anything other than well-proved building types.

3.38 The Parker-Morris standards adopted in Britain in 1967 led to spatial improvements in new housing, but rising costs and a national reluctance to pay more than the minimum for the roof over our heads has resulted in a decline in domestic building quality. The world-wide trend towards a 'throw-away' society, in which it is more popular to renew than repair, has had a detrimental effect upon domestic architecture. In order to arrest this process should we perhaps consider using a larger amount of our national resources to achieve better quality building at a higher initial cost, with a consequent reduction in the need for early replacement?

Building Land

3.39 Any sensible policy for the environment can only succeed if we stop pretending that our land supply is inexhaustible, and use our most valuable commodity in a more parsimonious way. Logically, therefore, it must be made more difficult for virgin land to be developed, despite the continuous pressure from an increasing population. The use of surplus railway land for building should be stepped up. For example, Marylebone Goods Yard, bought by Westminster City Council in 1966, will provide new homes for 5,000 people. More derelict land should be reclaimed, as in Durham, where over 7,600 acres will eventually have new uses for housing, recreation, and agriculture. At Sherburn Hill, we visited the area where a huge tip has been levelled and reclaimed for pasture land. Finished in 1971, the cost was £105,000. In Swansea also, the Council are levelling coal tips as a founda-tion for new schools. Despite the particular difficulties of reclamation redundant dockland in London presents a vast opportunity for new housing, and St Katherine-by-the-Tower, with its mixture of public and private housing, shops, restaurants and a yacht marina, will revitalise twenty two acres of Tower Hamlets.

overpage: Marygate Development, Royal Burgh of Pittenweem, Fife.

below: Model of Proposed Scheme for St Katherine-by-the-Tower, London.

Old Housing

3.40 The social problems and the environmental damage caused by large scale redevelopment schemes have led to increased interest in the rehabilitation of older housing districts. The London Boroughs of Islington and Hackney, for example, have positive policies to achieve this, helped by recent legislation. The fact that people can have new bathrooms, kitchens and other modern amenities, yet stay in the same area and often in the same house, prevents the uncertainties and often deep unhappiness when they are obliged to move away and break ties of family and friendship. One of the difficulties is that older dwellings are often occupied by the type of householder least able financially to help himself. Private owners or investors are sometimes reluctant to improve older homes because it is difficult to obtain a reasonable financial return. The greatest burden of rehabilitation is thrust upon local authorities, who have often found it both easier and more rewarding financially to knock down a whole area and start again from scratch.

3.41 A major problem of rehabilitation is that it results in an immediate increase in rateable value. This is apparently unavoidable under the present rating system. We feel that rate increases after improvements should be delayed for a five-year period, or until a change of ownership. This could prevent many older housing areas being allowed to deteriorate until total redevelopment becomes the only solution.

3.42 We have visited many towns and cities where local authorities have designated Housing Improvement Areas. In Middlesbrough the Teesside Corporation have a ten-year programme to improve 1,000 houses a year. We saw new bungalows for old people which have been cleverly inserted behind modernised 1930 period family homes. Coventry are rehabilitating a former estate of miners' houses and have let old allotment land at the rear for private building to ensure a mixed community. The Holyland area of Liverpool will be improved and not demolished due to pressure from residents themselves, and the Arlington Scheme at Norwich is a delightful example of small old houses saved to provide ideal accommodation for young couples.

3.43 But if we are to benefit from improvement and conservation of the nation's stock of existing houses, we must ensure that there are real and lasting financial incentives as compared with once and for all grants. We believe that there is a strong case for temporary rate relief for improved housing, coupled with re-examination of local government housing finance to ensure that towns do not suffer a progressive decline in income due to such an incentive. In financial terms, it should be made easier to improve existing houses than to build new ones, or at the very least, rehabilitation and rebuilding should be put on an equal footing.

The Brunton Hall, Musselburgh, Scotland.
The Raith Housing Estate, Kirkcaldy, Fife. Winner of Civic Trust Award.

New Housing

3.44 Where rehabilitation is impractical, it is still vital to take positive steps to stem the exodus from town centres. Obviously this means re-introducing housing into existing central areas, not as monolithic residential districts but as mixed developments. William Blake House in Soho, built by Westminster City Council, combines fifty flats, two floors of offices, a car park and an old peoples' club in a compact scheme. Alternatively, housing can be sensitively inserted into the existing pattern of a country town.

3.45 In Cirencester, Gloucestershire, 'The Triangle' development provides thirty eight bungalows and family homes in a traffic-free enclosure, linked to older modernised houses by small courts like St. Clements Walk. The gabled roofs, the soft colours of the North Cerney Chisledressed Bradstone, the careful detailing of lamps and landscaping blend perfectly with the early stone houses which are such a feature of this historic town. The land was in about twenty different ownerships and the local authority needed time and patience to achieve this excellent result. The easy way out would have been to build on land on the outskirts of the town, but this would simply have increased the very problem they were trying to solve.

3.46 There are plans for careful insertion of new housing in Hastings, Sussex, and many other local authorities are beginning to realise that people will return to live in towns and cities provided that both council and private housing is made more attractive, and when the immediate surroundings are congenial and convenient for the pursuit of work and leisure. The City of London's Barbican scheme, although over-powering in scale, is a step in the right direction. A town or city which is dead at night is only half-alive.

Housing Associations

3.47 Non-profit making Housing Associations will have an ever more important part to play in the overall housing pattern, but costs are often daunting, and in 1970 the Greater London Council set aside £25m a year for five years for loans to Housing Associations to try and solve this problem in the London area.

3.48 We were impressed by the Cockaigne Housing Association scheme at Hatfield. The twenty eight houses of highly original one-storey architecture, tiny interior courtyards and walled gardens give an impression of space on what is in reality a restricted site. Their adjacent social club provides a meeting place for people in the area. It also has a guestroom which can be hired out to relations or visitors. Bourneville Village Trust, Warwickshire, have a continuing programme for family housing, and the South Wales and Monmouthshire Association has in recent years provided over 1,000 homes for people in Cardiff. We feel there is a big potential for the work of the National Federation of Housing Societies in the provision of houses to let, to bridge the gap between private and local authority housing.

3.49   The necessity for high densities in cities has so often been given as an excuse for building ever more high-rise flats. The open space released around them usually turned out to be useless, since mothers were understandably afraid to let small children play unattended fifteen floors below them, and miserable windswept concrete areas could hardly be described as adventure playgrounds for older boys and girls. Low densities of 50 or 75 persons to the acre undoubtedly result in very attractive layouts, with low-built houses or flats and a lot of greenery, which is difficult to achieve in crowded city centres.

3.50   We feel that an entirely new approach to the design of flats is needed to provide a more attractive environment. Seven or eight storeys seem to be the highest now acceptable by the majority of people. Many local authorities have a policy of reserving point blocks for single people or couples with no children. But why are the surroundings of flats so often grim and cheerless? In one northern town, we visited the Council showpiece, a huge group of three and four storey flats for both families and old people. On one side, there was a manicured lawn decorated with one solitary tree. There were no seats, no shrubs, no animals, and in the early evening no people to be seen, only two boys kicking a ball in a desultory fashion on a concrete play area. Jane Jacobs would have despaired. When we commented on this lack of life we were told that people were not encouraged to walk on the grass as they might wear it out.

Social Facilities

3.51   In new housing developments, local authority schemes start with the advantage that many of the people housed have connections with the area since they are on the local housing list, and there is probably a sense of community which need not disappear as a result of a move if social facilities are readily available. Larger cities which have special slum clearance problems are sometimes rehousing residents at the rate of five or six thousand a year. Their priority is to provide a better standard of accommodation for as many people as quickly as possible. This has resulted in new houses being built rapidly and families moving in when the paint is barely dry. The different elements of a housing scheme can then get out of step.

3.52   Schools, for example, usually involve longer building programmes than houses, and their provision in recent years has suffered through government restraints on local authority spending. After a move children may have to travel long distances to attend schools near their previous homes. Shops may only appear a year or more after a large number of people have been housed; grass, trees and shrubs are rarely provided soon enough. In one large city we found that people in new homes have for nearly five years looked out on to boarded-up slums and acres of rubble. If people

are forced to live on what is virtually a building site during a very unsettled period in their domestic lives, severe social problems can arise, particularly when the general discomfort is coupled with the removal of ties with another district.

3.53 It seems clear that incentives must be offered and new arrangements made, to ensure that in any local authority housing scheme social facilities are provided and instant landscaping is installed in step with the provision of housing. There is a valuable lesson to be learned from Stevenage New Town where some 30,000 trees were planted during the initial stages of development and shrubs and trees are continually renewed. Today twenty years have passed and there is a wealth of greenery and mature trees everywhere.

Maintenance

3.54 In some developments, we felt that the cleanliness and general maintenance of the estates left a lot to be desired. A number of housing authorities receive continual complaints about external and internal maintenance. Internally, heaters, lights, lavatories, can easily go wrong, yet any private householder knows only too well the difficulty of persuading plumbers or electricians to come immediately; how much more difficult for a local authority with a stock of many thousands of dwellings. Would it not be better to allow tenants a discount on their rent if they were prepared to cope with their own internal repairs, leaving the local authority to concentrate on the external maintenance?

3.55 One new development virtually untried in Britain is the co-operative management of housing estates. Numerous public housing authorities in the United States hand over the running of the estates to elected tenants associations or co-operatives who look after common services, provide social facilities, take responsibility for the upkeep of the estate, draw up their own rules and regulations and even levy their own service charges. Not only is the housing authority relieved of the burden of maintaining and running the estate, but there is no doubt the residents themselves take a far greater interest in its appearance and well-being than is otherwise the case. We feel studies should be undertaken at once into the application of the co-operative principle to local authority housing in Britain.

Flexibility

3.56 Among the contributions made to the Working Party, the Planning Officer of Islington suggested that housing should be designed from the outset with alterations in mind. This is a most interesting idea. The needs of the householder vary at different periods of his life. Why not make allowance for this in housing design, since people are often unwilling to move to achieve the extra space? Prefabricated living-room extensions, bathroom or

Old People's Flats at Broomfield Green. Liverpool City Council. Civic Trust Award 1960.

pp. 54, 55: Aerial view of connecting courts in "The Triangle", Cirencester.

kitchen units are already widely used. Could this idea be elaborated to cover the problem of the middle-aged whose children may have left home to follow their own lives, and who might welcome houses which had detachable rooms?

3.57   A great deal has been talked about flexibility and in 1952 the then Ministry of Housing and Local Government pioneered some research into the matter. Further investigations have been carried out by Buckingham County Council and the National Building Agency, and both the Royal Institute of British Architects and the Huddersfield Building Society have run competitions for ideas on expandable homes. To date, technical limitations seem to have inhibited any major progress. We feel that further research should be done in this field.

Architecture

3.58   Architects are always annoyed by what they feel is uninformed criticism of their work, but they should accept the fact that it is a subject about which people feel they too are experts—like football or driving. What young man at the wheel of a souped-up second-hand car does not feel himself to be an embryonic winner of the Monte Carlo Rally, and what older man watching 'Match of the Day', does not feel that he could have kicked that winning goal?

3.59   'Mediocre, appalling, inhuman, banal and boring', are only a few of the adjectives used by our contributors to describe modern architecture as seen by people in towns and cities all over the country. The instant reaction is seldom wrong about architecture or people. The fact that people cannot explain precisely in architectural terms what is wrong does not necessarily make the building right.

3.60   We were frankly depressed during the course of our visits to see the damage wrought to towns and cities in the name of progress. A huge slab block which might look reasonable in Brasilia or set against the hills of Hong Kong can look totally incongruous towering over attractive Edwardian buildings at Mancastle-on-Trent. Or a supermarket which would be unnoticed in the outskirts of Los Angeles, can totally destroy the scale of the Georgian cottages at Little-Puddleton-in-the-Marsh.

3.61   Yet is this only the fault of architects? Who gave permission to erect such architecture? Some local authorities would argue that they are not justified in refusing planning permission for buildings just because they think they are ugly. And who can be the judge of ugliness? Yet the 1947 Planning Act gave powers to control siting, density, plot ratio, and design. How often have these limitations been compromised at the utterance of the magic words: 'Rateable Values'?

3.62   We have seen a block of flats in Wales built on a high ridge which dominates the town, when a lower site would have been visually acceptable, but doubtless more difficult for the architect and more expensive for the developer. New hotels in London too numerous to mention, have destroyed squares and shattered whole areas of low scale residential streets by their huge bulk. In other cities the centre has often been gutted to provide sites for concrete offices or large shopping precincts beside which the Victorian Town Hall, or the Georgian Art Gallery, left behind as a sop to tradition, look alienated and completely out of place.

3.63   We do not suggest that local authorities should have ignored the needs of twentieth-century living, or the economic advantages of our thriving tourist industry. We do suggest that they should have refused applications again and again until they were satisfied beyond reasonable doubt that the architecture would make a positive contribution to the environment. If the developers had gone away in disgust, let them go. There are many other developers who have a sensitive and responsible regard for our towns and cities, and they are still in business.

3.64　However, if a planning application is refused, there might be an appeal. Some council officers have told us that where they have refused applications in order to preserve the environment, they have subsequently lost on appeal. In these cases they have not been backed up by the Department of the Environment or the former Ministry of Housing and Local Government. We suggest that if the Secretary of State for the Environment wishes to encourage conservation and improvement that he should send a circular to every local planning authority asking them to interpret the existing Planning Acts for the maximum protection and enhancement of the habitat.

3.65　Although we are stuck with the slab blocks and the monolithic offices for many years to come, the picture is not one of unrelieved gloom and despondency. We have found in our travels a new awareness among local authorities of the importance of the total picture; that a point block here or a bulky building there can be a disaster, but that in the right places the difficult but necessary attachments to modern life such as air terminals, power stations or factories, can be cleverly sited to cause the least offence.

3.66　However this does not excuse inferior design. Several contributors have suggested architectural competitions, which are at an all-time low in this country, although widely used abroad. Others have mentioned the conflicts which can arise from the existing professional divisions between architects, planners, and engineers. This will be further discussed in our section on Education but is a matter worth investigation by the relevant professional associations.

3.67　Looking round, we have also seen some beautiful modern buildings, many of which have won Civic Trust awards, others which either by originality, elegance, or paradoxically by their very understatement, have made a positive contribution to their surroundings. To mention only a few: in Swansea, the Welsh Glass Works, of blue bricks, aluminium and glass, with a stepped frontage line and a free-standing curved internal staircase, is a stunning success. Coventry's public swimming baths, seen from the adjacent gardens or from the elevated roadway, are unusually attractive with a butterfly roof. Cockenzie Power Station, in Scotland, deserves its Civic Trust award by its restrained simplicity and cleverly sunken site.

3.68　Houses at Woodeaton near Oxford, in rough hewn Bradstone; the porphyry-coloured mosaic finish and Aztec-inspired motifs on new flats in the Gorbals, Glasgow; and the multi-storey car park in Wigmore Street, London, above a restaurant and shops with graceful arched windows, are all architecturally pleasing in different ways. Cathedrals or great houses are seldom commissioned nowadays. It is the everyday buildings which influence the character of a town, and by which, as Kenneth Clark writes, we will be judged by posterity.

Recommendations

7   *The Government should offer additional financial incentives to encourage rehabilitation and environmental improvements in older housing areas; and to encourage the return of a resident population to the centres of our towns and cities.*

8   *The Government should give extra financial encouragement for the improvement of individual dwellings, and rate increases on improved houses should be delayed for five years.*

9   *The development of virgin land should be more strictly controlled, especially where there is derelict or under-utilised land in urban areas.*

10   *The Government should give new incentives to ensure that social facilities and landscaping are provided to coincide with the completion of new housing projects.*

11   *The architectural profession should instigate further research into the design of homes which could be easily expanded or contracted according to the changing needs of the occupants.*

12   *Architectural competitions should be encouraged.*

13   *We suggest that the Secretary of State for the Environment sends a circular to all local planning authorities urging them to interpret the existing Planning Acts for the maximum protection and enhancement of the habitat.*

4 Conservation Areas and Historic Buildings

Contents

Public Opinion   63

Working Party Opinion   69

Introduction   69

Town Studies   70

Conservation Areas   71

Infilling and Rebuilding   75

Cleaning   75

Traffic   80
Foot Streets

Council Structure   81

Ownership and Finance   85
Historic Buildings Trusts
Tax Rebates
Death Duties

Conclusion   92

Recommendations   96

4 Public Opinion

4.1 **Rayleigh Civic Society** Sussex
'*We must keep historic buildings. They are irreplaceable, generally beautiful and often unique. Their neglect is inexcusable and their destruction is criminal.*'

4.2 **Henry Golding** St Ives, Cornwall
'*All over the realm the conservationists and the Civic Trusts are resolved to defend our priceless heritage to the last green field.*'

4.3 **St Fagan's Village Association** Wales
'*We must eradicate such television-reporter English as "preservationists" and "conservationists" both of which bring a vision of a tweed clad elderly lady intent on stopping everything which doesn't personally suit her.*'

4.4 **The Burton St Leonards Society** Sussex
'*I believe that the conservation movement is an expression of the concern that material progress should not be self-defeating.*'

4.5 **Civic Society of St Ives** Huntingdon
'*Our members want to preserve the character of the town without putting it in a straitjacket.*'

4.6 **The Aylsham Association**
'*There is no sense in conservation for the sake of conservation, it must have some ultimate worthwhile purpose.*'

4.7 **City of Coventry** Terence Gregory, City Architect and Planning Officer
'*If valued buildings and environment from the past are ruthlessly destroyed it can result in a feeling that there are no roots or anchors in urban society.*'

4.8 **Heavy Lorries** A Civic Trust Report, Extract
'*Before commencing the present enquiry the Civic Trust was aware that a certain amount of damage was being done to historic buildings by heavy lorries which collided with them. As many as 25% of the societies replying to the Trust's letter cited cases in which damage of this kind had actually occurred, and the proportion was alarmingly higher in historic towns listed by the Council for British Archaeology—39%.*'

4.9 **Urban District Councils Association**

'Is it essential to keep historic buildings? It may be desirable—in some cases more desirable than others, but as a nation we must be careful not to be living on the past. Other nations may well encourage us to live on our past and our past includes the preservation of old buildings and with them old habitats, and whilst we are doing this other nations progress in modern and obviously more profitable forms.'

4.10 **The Midhurst Society** Sussex

'The difficulty is that we try to preserve too much; no place that is dead or dying is of interest to most people.'

4.11 **Angela Reynolds** Putney SW15

'Just behind the congestion and bustle of Putney High Street an interesting fan-shaped group of three cul-de-sacs provides a calm and pleasing environ-environment free from through traffic. Stratford Grove and Charlwood Terrace have small semi-detached villas dating from 1850, while Lifford Street consists of smaller terraced houses built about 1870. The houses are unpretentious but have considerable charm and are of good proportion. When we first suggested that it be designated a conservation area we were unaware that the threat of redevelopment hung over one of the streets. The original desire was to protect an area with a charm and quality worth preserving. Later, we fought to keep intact the close-knit community. With the help of the GLC and Wandsworth Borough Council our campaign succeeded and the streets are now designated as a conservation area. Designation has given the residents new hope and has increased their pride in their streets.'

4.12 **Haslemere Estates Ltd** F E Cleary

'Each local authority should set up a committee charged with the sole purpose of improving the environment of their city, town, borough, or county. Very few local authorities have such a committee. In the City of London we do have one, but it has only been formed two or three years ago. Generally matters of environment or amenity get tacked onto the end of the Town Planning or Works Committee or Parks Committee agenda, and there is never really time to give any thought to such items.'

4.13 **London Borough of Merton** Town Clerk

'In conservation areas measures are urgently needed to protect "unlisted buildings" which perhaps of little architectural value in themselves, nevertheless play an important part in the townscape. A number of measures are possible—placing the onus on an owner to prove for specific reasons the building must be demolished; to include "demolition", in definition of "development" in the Planning Acts 1962-68; the use of "Article 4" directions restricting permitted development in selected areas; and the

possible introduction of tax concessions in recognition of the preservation of buildings.'

4.14 Weald of Kent Preservation Society
'The economics of preservation should be put on a national basis. Why should the taxpayer support say, five thousand listed buildings in our county where the taxpayer in an adjacent county has to support only five hundred?'

4.15 Margate Civic Society Kent
'Tax concessions should be allowed to owners of listed buildings, for maintenance and improvements and also by way of death duty exemption.'

4.16 Weymouth Civic Society Dorset
'There should be a Council for Historic Towns for the purpose of financing conserved districts.'

4.17 National Federation of Housing Societies
'Housing Associations are already active in both these fields. We have purchased a number of historic buildings, improved them into self-contained flats and then let at a non-profit rent. Nevertheless such rents are generally considerably higher than local average and this has often caused a political stir locally in that public money has been used to provide housing that can only be rented to higher income group people. If policy was clear that the prime purpose was to preserve the environment and that the housing provision was secondary, but financially the only way to secure that preservation, then we could be much more active.'

4.18 Association of Municipal Corporations
'It is considered that listed buildings in towns are part of the national heritage and that the national purse should make a greater contribution to their preservation than is now made. Full use of available grants, including substantial grants from the local authority itself, can still leave a substantial balance required which owners may not be in a position to pay.'

4.19 The Bruton Trust Somerset
'We find through rather sad experience that we are entirely dependent on self-help as Somerset is a poor county with many worthy buildings to preserve and no money with which to do the job.'

4.20 Council for the Preservation of Rural England
'A national lottery might raise money for all forms of conservation. Prizes might be in the form of grants to areas chosen by the winners.'

4.21 **National Trust for Scotland**
'A new approach was developed—a "revolving fund". This means that the Trust buys a house, restores it, sells it under safeguards, and uses the money to repeat the operation with another property. Now, after ten years in the East Neuk of Fife alone, over sixty properties have been or are being restored work on hand at a recent calculation totalled £115,000.'

4.22 **London Borough of Wandsworth** Director of Development
'Often there is a reluctance to accept older converted buildings for education or welfare uses because of financial inflexibility, but if additional maintenance and running costs could be charged to some sort of preservation account, such conversions might more often be justified.'

4.23 **Country Landowners Association**
'Anxieties are now greater for the less important but no less beautiful homes which form such an important part of the English scene. Even if they are open to the public, their size, situation or arrangements usually make this activity unviable; their taxation treatment is unfavourable; and the Historic Buildings Council has often had to refuse grants in all but the most outstanding cases through lack of funds.

4.24 **Conservation in the Development of Northern Ireland** Study Group 2. 1970
'As building techniques become more uniform throughout the world, we must try to retain regional character as expressed by the countryside, village, townscape and handicrafts. A plan must be developed for the total conservation of outstanding areas, groups of works, whole villages or areas, the properties being conserved in their setting. Features such as craft workshops, fine farm buildings, nature trails, history trails, wildfowl collections, local museums, etc. must be developed or restored so that a total cultural and recreational experience is provided.'

4.25 **Bath, a Study in Conservation** Extract from the conclusions **Colin Buchanan and Partners 1968**
'We took it as axiomatic that conservation did not imply preservation in the museum sense, but rather the retention, and where necessary enhancement, of all that is architecturally and historically valuable together with the maintenance of the areas as a setting for normal vigorous urban life. The quintessence of the conservation problem concerns buildings and layouts which are valuable for their own sake, but which are no longer suitable for contemporary use. This general unsuitability for present day use and the lack of a profit motive to encourage developers or others to adapt premises for suitable uses, leads to property lying vacant and then to physical decay. The problem is to reverse this process, even if there be a financial loss, to find new uses for the buildings, to deal with the traffic, and to arrest the decay. Conservation is bound to involve preservation but it is more than preservation it is bringing an area back to life.'

4.26 **The Countess of Dartmouth** former Chairman of Greater London Council Historic Buildings Board, Extract from "Do You Care about Historic Buildings" 1970

'Last autumn I went to a seminar on historic buildings held in London. Taking part were architects from Australia, America and Canada. I expected to have to argue the case for preservation. Not at all—I was able to sit almost silent while eminent architects from newer countries pleaded with us to keep our historic buildings.

Surely we can keep a balance between old and new? In the last few years there has been a quickly growing interest in the preservation of historic buildings, a movement towards the conservation of trees, birds, plants and environment. Max Nicholson in "The Environmental Revolution" showed us how man can elevate and then destroy himself and his surroundings. One of the easiest ways to achieve this end is to start by destroying our historic buildings. With the passing of each one goes a slice of social history—a thread of civilisation. Surely we can learn to reweave those threads in a bright new context, so that our children and grandchildren can respond, as we have, to the challenge of beauty created hundreds of years ago.'

overpage: Restored Houses in New Street, Plymouth.

4 Working Party Opinion

Introduction

4.27 Conservationists used to be thought cranks. Today there are over 750 local amenity societies throughout the country, and people of all ages and income groups actively press for the preservation of Britain's 250,000 historic buildings. This movement is not just emotional, but based on logic. Thousands of nineteenth century terraced houses have been modernised to provide homes at lower cost than new construction; mansions have become offices, where gilded ceilings or wall-paintings by Angelica Kaufmann soothe the nerves of busy directors; and countless tourists contribute to our economy by their visits to historic towns.

4.28 Nowadays it is generally realised that buildings cannot be considered in isolation. Groups of attractive old houses and shops give charm and character to an area, and their destruction often means toothless gaps in the street pattern. Sympathetic infilling can modify the loss, but thoughtless modern alternatives can be a disaster.

4.29 Many worthwhile buildings have been lost by a mistake. In some cases they were unlisted; in other cases the notice of listing was not served on the owner in time to prevent demolition; and before the stricter laws in the 1968 Town and Country Planning Acts, owners who demolished or deliberately allowed historic buildings to fall down, could only be fined a maximum of £100.

4.30 Much of this has been put right. Georgian buildings have for a long time been both fashionable and cherished, but the merit is now increasingly recognised of Victorian, Edwardian, Art Nouveau, and notable architecture erected after 1900: amenity societies are up in arms if there are rumours that local buildings may be demolished; and philistine owners can face Building Repair Notices, acquisition by the local authority at minimum compensation, stiff fines, and even prison.

4.31 Yet buildings can still slip through the legal net; and badly designed car parks, shops or offices, as well as council-operated Traffic Management Schemes, can ruin entire historic areas. It is therefore vital to look at cities, towns and villages as a whole. First we should find out what exists which merits preservation and improvement, consider the problems of restoration and maintenance, both dependent upon finance, and then assess the role of old buildings in the human habitat of the twentieth century.

Town Studies

4.32   We were particularly impressed by a town study of Faversham, in Kent. 'Faversham Conserved' sets out the problems, the aims, the solutions, and identifies the individual values of their many historic houses, courts and lanes. Over the years, the Borough Council have carefully acquired land for car parking in preparation for pedestrianising certain streets, and have already applied in accordance with recent Government policy, for funds to enable them to build a by-pass. This will syphon off the heavy lorries and container traffic which constantly endanger their buildings.

4.33   Houses are being continually painted and rehabilitated, sometimes by means of Housing Improvement Grants; planning applications are studied in relation to the whole, and we found that both members and officers of the Borough Council, private owners, and Kent County Council, were actively engaged in preserving and improving buildings with regard to the economic and commercial life of the town. All this would have been difficult, if not impossible, without a thorough survey.

4.34   In 1968, the Government commissioned studies of four famous historic towns—Chichester, York, Bath and Chester. York, which attracts over three quarters of a million tourists a year, has severe traffic problems, and a wealth of beautiful old buildings needing considerable finance for restoration. Recently we saw many houses in Stonegate and Petergate newly restored and used as shops or flats; York Civic Trust have erected a magnificent fountain in front of the Art Gallery, and foot streets are attracting more shoppers to the historic areas. There are plans for Bath which include an £8 million traffic tunnel under the main Georgian core, and further proposals in the studies will be implemented for the other historic towns.

4.35   Bury St Edmunds have an interesting survey prepared by the Suffolk Preservation Society, which underlines the need to preserve the human scale in all redevelopment of this medieval town, where the Norman street pattern is still visible. In contrast, a study of the De Beauvoir area of Hackney, in London, just behind the busy Kingsland Road, leading to the docks, highlighted the many early nineteenth century houses which were sadly in need of care. In a more fashionable area, they would have been snapped up for good prices, but a concerted effort was needed to restore them. The Borough Council gave a lead by entirely rehabilitating a show house complete with new bathroom, kitchen and heating by means of the Housing Improvement Grants which offer owners up to £1,000 a house, or £1,500 in certain areas for modernisation, if they spend an equal sum. The scheme was highly successful, over forty houses have already been completely refurbished, and Hackney also received enquiries from all over the country.

Conservation Areas

4.36   Since the Civic Amenities Act of 1967, promoted by Duncan Sandys MP, founder of the Civic Trust, there are now over 1,600 Conservation Areas in Great Britain. One of the most attractive we have seen is Pinner High Street, Harrow. The architecture is of all periods—the seventeenth century public house blending with Georgian, Victorian and mock Tudor. In 1964 the Borough Architect suggested ideas for improvement, and owners of shops, offices and houses agreed with the Council to contribute financially to an overall plan. Litter bins and the telephone kiosk were re-sited, ugly street furniture and unsightly advertisements removed. There are smart shop fronts, new paving, and lanterns on wall-brackets which provide attractive lighting. There are hanging baskets of flowers, seats, plants and gay paintwork. It is now a show place for Harrow.

4.37   The centre of Haddington is a fascinating example of a conservation area in Scotland. A variety of unusual buildings are dominated by the Georgian 'Town House'. There is the dutch-gabled shoe shop of 1650, sporting the sign of the Wellington boot; the chemist, hung with a gilded pestle and mortar, and the eighteenth century Old George Hotel with its curious Gothic turrets. Now repainted and modernised, the many old houses have attracted young professional people into the town. Parking and rear access for shops has been cleverly organised, and the result is an economic and aesthetic success.

Norton Village Green, Co. Durham. Conservation Area.

4.38   Other delightful examples of conservation areas are Norton, Co Durham
        which has the pond as a focal point; Sowerby, Yorkshire, with its man
        Georgian cottages; and Mumbles, Wales, where tiny twisting lanes lead t
        the boat-filled shores of Swansea Bay. But it is essential to have furthe
        protection of unlisted buildings in conservation areas. At present the Civ
        Amenities Act lacks teeth. For example, in a small village dependent fo
        its charm upon a group of buildings not good enough for the statutor
        lists, these could all disappear over-night.

4.39   New proposals for legislation before Parliament could make it necessar
        to obtain planning permission for all demolition in a conservation are
        but this would not prevent mutilation of buildings, such as cornice
        lopping. Alternatively, local authorities could draw up their own local lis
        of buildings which are important to their own particular area, but perhap
        not acceptable for Grade II listing. These local lists could be submitted t
        the Secretary of State, and the buildings would automatically require liste
        building consent under Part V of the 1968 Act, for alteration or demolition

p. 72: Lifford Street, Putney. Conservation Area.
p. 73: Mumbles Village Lane, Swansea, Wales. Conservation Area.

below: Infilling of shops in Llandaff High Street, Cardiff. Conservation Area.

p. 76: 36 Looe Street, Plymouth—before restoration.
p. 77: 36 Looe Street, Plymouth—after restoration.

Infilling and Rebuilding

4.40 A brash new supermarket or offices built regardless of the existing scale can so easily spoil groups of attractive buildings. We have visited many places where the street pattern has been wrecked by one large store which has replaced four or five small shops. New buildings in a conservation area, or near to historic buildings, must be in sympathy with existing architecture.

4.41 For example, the Jenny Lind housing scheme in Norwich, in soft red brick, is a great success on a small and difficult site. St Katharine Dock House, Tower Hamlets, respects the height and scale of the Telford warehouses; the infilling of four shops in Llandaff High Street, Cardiff, is done with great imagination; new undergraduates' rooms at Brasenose College, Oxford, cleverly harmonise with existing buildings dating from the fifteenth to the late nineteenth century; while Brighton Square, with its small shops, restaurants, seats, plants, and atmosphere of continental gaiety, is exactly the right complement to the famous Lanes. We saw well designed old people's flats in Bloomfield Green, facing Sefton Park, in Liverpool; their modest but elegant architecture, in the Georgian style, certainly deserved their Civic Trust award. In the Barbican area of Plymouth, new buildings in Castle Street and Lambhay Hill marry up with the many restored Elizabethan houses by the use of local stone, cobbled pavements, small connecting courts, and a careful choice of street furniture.

4.42 On a larger scale we were greatly impressed by the new shopping precinct at Salisbury, Wiltshire. Three historic streets, with a mixture of seventeenth and eighteenth century buildings, have been entirely restored and modernised. New additions respect the existing height and scale of the unusual houses and shops, with their early tiles, mullioned windows, gables and attractive broken street pattern. The entrance to the precinct is beneath the blackbeamed fourteenth century Old George Hotel, seemingly supported by huge wooden pillars, which hide the necessary steel joists, and the corner shops have curved bay windows in the manner of the eighteenth century. Canopies faced with hardwood and roofed with old tiles protect shoppers from wind and rain; there are seats and tubs of flowers, and the Mall leads through rows of modern shops to the central area where you find the supermarket and Marks and Spencer. Behind lie the carefully sited service areas and a carpark for 650 cars. This excellent development is a perfect marriage between old and new, done by private enterprise in close co-operation with the local authorities.

Cleaning

4.43 During our many visits round the country we noticed with pleasure the remarkable effect of a wash and brush-up on historic buildings. Visitors to France over the past few years constantly praise the visual delight of the Place Vendome, The Opera and the Madeleine. In London, the Albert Hall,

Entrance to shopping precinct through Old George Mall, Salisbury.

recently cleaned as a result of a national appeal, now dazzles all who pass by with its elaborate frieze representing the arts and sciences, the warm red brick and vast domed roof. The General Register House, Edinburgh, by Robert Adam, gives a stunning impression, and the honey-coloured stone of Christ Church College, Oxford, among many other pristine buildings in that city, is perhaps the most outstanding. Councillors in Leeds are considering whether to clean at an estimated cost of £40,000 their magnificent town hall, guarded by stone lions, the whole pillared structure blackened by years of pollution. The Lord Provost of Glasgow has recently announced plans for a 'Face-Lift' for buildings in 1972, and the elegant Stock Exchange in Buchanan Street, reminiscent of a Doge's Palace, already sets a shining example.

4.44   To encourage a real clean-up of our towns and cities, we think that every new District Council should establish a cleaning fund with money set aside each year from the rates for cleaning both public and privately owned buildings. Percentage grants to owners could help achieve this. In London the Government have given a lead by cleaning, among other buildings, Inigo Jones' Banqueting House in Whitehall, Buckingham Palace, and the National Gallery, which, lit up at night or seen behind a swirl of pigeons and the soaring fountains of Trafalgar Square, is a focal point for tourists and Londoners.

Christ Church Library, Oxford—before restoration.

Christ Church Library, Oxford—after restoration.

Traffic

4.45 The greatest threat to conservation areas, historic buildings, and histor towns and villages, is undoubtedly traffic. Mobility is one of the outstand ing advantages of our century, and no-one would want to turn our tow and villages into lifeless museums, to ignore a shopper's need to arrive b car or bus, or to strangle trade and commerce by unnecessary restriction But the Civic Trust report on 'Heavy Lorries', the horrifying evidence irreparable damage to small towns on a through route to the coast major city, proves the necessity of definite traffic policies which can strik the correct balance.

4.46 When we spent an afternoon in Thirsk, a pleasant market town in York shire which has some fine buildings, police twice had to clear the entir street to allow huge articulated lorries to inch their way round the corner of old houses, and the appalling noise made conversation in the stre almost impossible. Tenterden, an unusually attractive old town in Kent suffers from endless container traffic going through to the coast; the narro streets of Ludlow, in Shropshire, with many medieval black-beamed house and shops, echo to the noise of lorries en route to Wales; and we watche vans and lorries rattle round the twisting streets of Horsham in Susse Newbury, in Berkshire, where there are many historic buildings, was ofte choked with traffic of all kinds until their North-South relief road wa built, which takes away the heavy traffic travelling from the Midlands t Southampton.

Members of Working Party and Officials at Tenterden, Kent.

4.47   In the Spring of 1971 the Government announced that special account would be taken of the needs of historic towns in allocating money for by-passes. This is of major importance because it will not only mean the removal of heavy traffic from town centres, but create new environmental opportunities. In Tewkesbury, Gloucestershire, where the completion of a nearby stretch of the M5 has syphoned off much heavy traffic, the town centre has been revived. In many towns upper storeys of historic houses are unused and fast deteriorating, because living conditions have become impossible with the noise and fumes of passing vehicles. Stamford, in Lincolnshire, where trade increased in several streets when the North-South by-pass was finished in 1962, now urgently needs an East-West by-pass to take away the traffic going from the Fens to the Midlands. Meantime, we saw lorries mounting the pavements to get round the corners of the narrow streets, endangering the many beautiful houses which date from medieval times.

Foot Streets

4.48   The establishment of foot streets has resulted in the protection and improvement of many historic buildings. In London Street, Norwich, shops and banks have been newly painted in a variety of gay colours, and trees, seats and kiosks replace the traffic. In the foot streets of Leeds, newly listed Edwardian buildings blackened by over sixty years of pollution, turn out when cleaned to be of dazzling salmon pink stone, sometimes inlaid with golden mosaics; and the magnificent nineteenth century Renaissance style buildings in Buchanan Street, Glasgow, will have a face-lift when plans for pedestrianisation are implemented in the coming year.

Council Structure

4.49   We would like to suggest improvements which could be made in the structure of local government to promote further interest and action for conservation areas and historic buildings. One of our contributors makes the point that in some councils questions of conservation are tacked on to the end of planning committees when members are tired and want to get away. The Greater London Council has a Historic Buildings Board to deal specifically with this subject. It is a sub-committee of Environmental Planning. There are sixteen members, twelve from the Council, six co-opted as advisors. In many towns and cities there are members of amenity and antiquarian societies who have a wide knowledge of buildings and architecture; there is often the Chamber of Commerce and other important groups who are anxious to effect improvements to the town. We feel there would be many volunteers for such an interesting task.

4.50   We therefore suggest that each council should set up a Conservation and Improvements Sub-Committee, with its own budget allocated from the planning vote. Their terms of reference would be to undertake a town study, if none exists; to think up positive improvements, to deal with all

The Town Hall Manchester, *built by Alfred Waterhouse.*

St Martin-at-Palace Plain, Norwich—before restoration.

St Martin-at-Palace Plain, Norwich—after restoration.

Church House, Clare, Suffolk.

Restored with grant from Historic Buildings Council.

applications concerning the demolition, alteration or improvement of historic buildings including infilling in conservation areas, and to give their opinion to the main committee on all planning applications which could affect conservation.

4.51 We are worried by one aspect of the new legislation on local government reform. The new District Councils will have responsibility for historic buildings but in this field there is a serious lack of trained and experienced staff. Some County Councils have built up expert teams, and one way of meeting this problem would be by District Councils appointing those qualified teams as their agents. There is also a distinct shortage of architectural courses in the techniques of restoration and conversion. As the future of many old buildings entirely depends upon their intelligent and sympathetic conversion to an up-to-date use, the situation could become grave.

Ownership and Finance

4.52 The majority of historic buildings in this country are privately owned; others belong to local authorities, the Government or the Church. But whatever we would ideally like to do in the field of conservation there is always the problem of finance.

4.53 On the advice of the Historic Buildings' Council, the Secretary of State for the Environment makes available to owners grants which now total £1m a year, for the repair and maintenance of buildings of outstanding historic or architectural interest in England. There are similar arrangements for Scotland and Wales. By this means many unique buildings have been saved. Town and country houses, ruins, early barns, or water mills, together form a chain of outstanding buildings which stretches right across Great Britain.

4.54 County Councils and Borough Councils can give grants to owners from various estimates. For example, in 1971 the Greater London Council set aside £25,000 a year from the Planning Vote and the Borough of Lambeth £5,000, while Islington voted £6,000 for 'General Amenity'. The Hastings County Borough Council, Sussex, have made grants totalling £1,000 to help owners of the many old buildings in the area including some town houses in St. Leonards-on-Sea, designed by James Burton in the 1830's.

4.55 It is difficult to compare the generosity of various councils without also giving numbers of listed buildings within their boundaries. Gloucestershire, for instance, has 7,686 buildings while Nottinghamshire has 1,385. Some ratepayers are more heavily burdened than others, while some councils are more interested in preservation than others.

4.56 Housing Improvement Grants, possible under the Housing Vote, have saved many attractive houses in conservation areas. About thirty two

towns have benefited from grants jointly paid by the Department of the Environment and local authorities through 'Town Schemes', which enable whole groups of buildings to be restored. But why not at least include the fifty-one towns listed by the Council of British Archaeology as being of national importance?

4.57   Historic buildings owned by local authorities are paid for from the rates and serve a useful purpose for education, recreation, the arts, council offices or sewage disposal. Wentworth Woodhouse, Yorkshire, by Henry Flitcroft, is a teacher training college; the former Corn Exchange in Gainsborough's home town of Sudbury, Suffolk, is a public library; seventeenth century alms-houses in Shoreditch are a children's museum; the Lord Mayor of Manchester reigns in a Town Hall which is a masterpiece of Victorian Gothic architecture, and sewage still passes through the pumping station at Abbey Mills, Newham, designed in 1865 in Venetian Gothic style by the great engineer Joseph Bazalgette.

4.58   The Crown own many historic buildings, and among the Crown Estate Commissioners' most exciting restorations are Carlton House Terrace and the Nash terraces in Regent's Park. Government Departments occupy other historic buildings such as the Treasury, Whitehall and Somerset House. These are maintained by the Department of the Environment and paid for out of public funds. Development by the Crown does not require planning permission, nor do Government Departments need listed building consent for alterations or demolition. From October 1971, local planning authorities are notified under Circular 80 of any proposed development, and within two months they can if necessary object, which could result in a public inquiry. Although this procedure is an improvement over the former Circular 100, it still seems that there is one law for the rulers and another for the ruled.

4.59   Many beautiful churches in this country are no longer needed for ecclesiastical use; some are finding a new, secular use, like St Mary-at-Quay, Ipswich, now occupied by the Boys' Brigade, or St Peters-in-the-East, Oxford, used as a library by St Edmunds Hall. Others will be cared for by the Redundant Churches Fund.

4.60   The most difficult cases are where historic houses are left empty and uncared for, and while generous grants might be available to help the owner, he has literally no money of his own to pay his share of the cost of repairs. Until repaired the house is unsaleable. There are also grave problems when an owner of a listed house of medium size is suddenly faced with dry rot or roof collapse which could cost several thousands of pounds. What can he do if unable to foot the bill? Unfortunately, councils are usually unwilling to use their discretionary powers under the Local Authorities Historic

Abbey Mills Pumping Station, Newham, London.

Buildings Act 1962 to give grants for repairs and maintenance. Yet our more modest historic houses are equally a part of our national heritage which should be retained.

Historic Buildings Trusts

4.61   We think there should be many more Historic Buildings Trusts. The National Trust is justly famous and has done magnificent work. The National Trust for Scotland has spent more than £200,000 on over forty Buildings, including those in their 'Little Houses' scheme, which has restored so much in the Neuk of Fife. At Pan-ha, in the old salt town of Dysart, we visited seventeenth century houses linked by a cobbled right of way which have been restored and now form a group with carefully designed new homes all having breath-taking views over the estuary of the Forth.

4.62   Both Trusts have endowment funds for many of their larger houses, raise money by subscriptions and other efforts, and receive substantial sums from the Government by remission of death duties or grants from the Historic Buildings Council.

4.63   There are about thirty other smaller trusts in different parts of the country. The trusts exist to buy historic buildings, repair them and then re-sell with protective covenants or let them on long leases. Plymouth Barbican Association have funds of £50,000, The Farnham Trust £10,000, and the Kings Lynn Preservation Trust, £186,000. These are only approximate figures, since some trusts retain their properties, others hold them only long enough to achieve their restoration before re-sale.

4.64   We strongly support the Civic Trust in their suggestion to the Department of the Environment that some 200 local trusts should be established, each with capital of not less than £25,000. A pound for pound grant or interest-free loan should be given by their local authorities towards funds which they could raise themselves. By this means at least 400 buildings a year could be saved. If these were resold when modernised and restored, or let on a ninety-nine year lease, the money could return to the trust and be used again.

4.65   We also urge that a National Buildings Conservation Fund should be set up for loans to trusts as a last resort, when local councils have already contributed, and the trusts are unable to raise more money. To establish this fund a capital sum of up to three million pounds would be required, and we suggest that the Government should help towards raising it.

St Peter's in the East, Oxford. Now a library for St Edmund Hall.

Sixteenth Century Building used by Lloyds Bank at Henley-in-Arden, Warwickshire.

Tax Rebates

4.66 The question of Tax Rebates for owners of listed buildings was discussed in a report to the Secretary of State in 1970, by the Preservation Policy Group, but they did not give the proposal priority in their recommendations. However we definitely favour tax rebates for repairs to listed houses too modest to attract a grant from the Historic Buildings Council. We also suggest that the rebate should not be allowed on the first two hundred pounds of money spent yearly on repairs, or six hundred pounds over three years, to allow for an owner's ordinary repair liability on any building in which he chooses to live.

Death Duties

4.67 We also think there is a case for remission of death duties in connection with historic buildings. If an article of accepted national artistic importance can be exempted from estate duty provided that it is kept in the United Kingdom, properly maintained, and made reasonably available for public inspection, why could not a similar system be worked out for houses of really first class national importance?

4.68 We have in mind buildings which are of such importance that, if their owners can no longer afford to maintain them, they would have to be taken over and supported by public funds in one way or another. It would be surely better and cheaper in the long run for public funds if these could be kept in the ownership of their families, so long as they kept the houses in good repair and allowed reasonable access to the public? Death duties would still be chargeable if the house were sold or the other conditions infringed.

4.69 We also suggest that there should be remission of death duties on smaller listed buildings donated outright to local Historic Buildings Trusts. We ask that both the question of tax rebates and death duties in relation to historic buildings be investigated without further delay.

top: Lavenham, Suffolk, before removal of overhead wires.

bottom: Lavenham, Suffolk, after removal of overhead wires.

Conclusion

4.70   Change is inevitable—but in places where all old buildings have been swept away people feel a sense of insecurity and the continuity is lost for ever. It is essential to keep some buildings of historic or architectural interest of all kinds and all periods—houses, windmills, warehouses, theatres, churches and even some railway stations, most of which can be converted to a modern use, whilst giving visual pleasure to visitors, residents or passers by.

4.71   The Civic Amenities Act of 1967 gave new hope to people struggling to keep intact groups of houses or shops whose loss could destroy the whole identity of their town or village. The stricter laws affecting historic buildings in Part V and Schedule V of the 1968 Town and Country Planning Act have saved many beautiful houses, and more and more local authorities realise the importance of revitalising their historic areas.

4.72   In the Department of the Environment a small but devoted team do much to make this possible. They service the Historic Buildings Council, advise local authorities on their problems; and it is their investigators who actually tramp the streets in order to survey and classify buildings of merit throughout the country before they compile the lists.

4.73   The Civic Trust cannot be praised too much. They have brought owners, local authorities and even conflicting interests together to improve and beautify streets, squares or town centres. Amenity societies have shown their determination to fight for what is precious in their own areas, and have become a new force in the land.

4.74   In the long run the beauty of Britain can only be protected by public opinion. We must remain on our guard to watch over historic buildings, large and small, which still seem to disappear too easily. We must all make individual efforts to keep the charm and character of our towns and villages for ourselves, our visitors, our grandchildren, and for many centuries to come.

Dirleton Village and Green, East Lothian. Conservation Area.

p. 94: Sussex Place, Regent's Park, before restoration by the Crown Commissioners.

p. 95: Sussex Place, Regent's Park, after restoration by the Crown Commissioners.

Recommendations

14   *We welcome the new proposals for legislation for the great* *protection of unlisted buildings in conservation areas.*

15   *Local authorities should follow the example of the Governme* *by establishing a Cleaning Fund for the regular cleaning* *public buildings; they should give owners percentage gran* *from this fund towards the cost of cleaning privately-own* *buildings.*

16   *Each local authority should set up a special sub-committee* *their planning committee with its own budget, to be concerne* *with conservation, historic buildings, and town improvements.*

17   *Suitable measures should be taken to increase the supply* *architects, builders and craftsmen with skills in the repair an* *adaptation of historic buildings.*

18   *The new District Councils should take urgent steps to obta* *skilled professional advice on the historic buildings whic* *will become their responsibility. In some cases they could us* *County Council staff as their agents. Under the act, th* *Secretary of State for the Environment should require Distri* *Councils to make arrangements which he considers to b* *satisfactory.*

19   *We also ask the Government to reconsider that part of the ne* *legislation which removes all historic buildings powers fro* *County Councils. There should however, be opportunities fo* *preservation at both levels of local government, provided tha* *the arrangements of the authorities concerned satisfy th* *Secretary of State.*

20   *More Historic Building Trusts, and a National Building* *Conservation Fund, should be established without delay.*

21   *The Government should consider the whole question of ta* *rebates and estate duty in relation to historic buildings.*

5 Traffic

Contents

Public Opinion 99

Working Party Opinion 103

Introduction 103

Urban Traffic 103
By-Passes
Environmental Management
Road Space
Parking

Public Transport 110

Pedestrians 111

Conclusion 115

Recommendations 116

5   Public Opinion

5.1   **R E Pahl**   Extract from **'Whose City'**

'Intellectuals are not sure whether the car must adapt to the city or the city to the car. Their attitude to the London motorway box seems to depend more on whether it affects their local area or whether they have recently been ensnarled in crawling traffic for hours, rather than on any clear vision of what the city might and should be.'

5.2   **The Richmond Society**   Surrey

'We can preserve and improve our habitat only if we control the element which is threatening its absolute destruction—motor traffic.'

5.3   **The Pedestrian Association for Road Safety**   Personal views of the Hon Consultant T C Foley

'Traffic should be separated from pedestrians. There should be more shopping precincts and streets from which wheeled traffic is excluded, and in particular, during busy hours of the day city centres should be reserved for pedestrians as far as possible. The car and the lorry are destroying the characteristics of a good and sympathetic environment in towns, and unless they are strictly controlled and limited in number urban life will be made intolerable, as indeed is already the case in many places.'

5.4   **Greater London Council**

'The Council's answer is a balanced package of investment in public transport; of restraint, by parking controls and management measures, including the creation of environmental areas freed from extraneous traffic; of the establishment of a hierarchy of urban roads to serve particular types of traffic, and of a relatively limited amount of new construction, particularly of urban motorways.'

5.5   **British Railways Board**

'In the Board's view, there is very great potential, in the large conurbations, for bettering living conditions by meeting transport needs by improving the existing, usually widespread, rail network. This can be achieved at a cost which will normally be modest, when compared with the road expenditure which would otherwise be needed.'

5.6   **The Aylsham Association**   Norfolk

'One may learn from experience at Godalming, Surrey, how to deal with car parks for shoppers. The site was based on the principle that if it is more than

150-200 yards away from the bulk of the shops, it would not willingly be used. A free car park was made behind the shops in the main and busy street with separate ways in and out. The convenience of this set-up attracted so many people to shop in the town that the car park had to be enlarged to four times its original capacity.'

5.7   **Ilkley Civic Society** Yorkshire
'Roads, as products of civil engineering, can be, and very often are, pleasing and well-designed—for example the Motorway network. With roads the adverse impact comes from the vehicles using the road themselves.'

5.8   **Dr Savage** Plymouth Devon
'Public transport must be more extensive and more imaginative than at present. Suggestions include the use of moving pavements in the city streets and mini-buses to serve districts from which it would not be economic to run the conventional large single and double-decker buses.'

5.9   **Peter Harris** Reading University
'The growing tendency for heavy commercial vehicles to be parked in residential areas constitutes a form of mobile pollution. They destroy the character of an area, are a danger to children born in motion and stationary, and create noise problems when moved at unreasonable hours.'

5.10   **The Automobile Association**
'The motor vehicles population explosion in Britain arises from a continuous increase in living standards and the desire of people to own a car, and the fact that some 90% of goods moved in servicing the community is now transported by road. We adopt a view which takes into account the greatest good of the community as a whole. We accept, therefore, that motorists should not have priority over everyone else in the use of their vehicles no matter what the consequences in environmental terms.
Experience in major cities all over the world demonstrates that the building of urban motorways is fundamental to an improvement in environment.'

5.11   **Peter Mason** Consulting Engineer
'In our city of the future, what differences shall we see? Multilevel traffic ways will be a fundamental feature. It must be accepted that, for a major city at any rate, unrestricted use of the private car will be an anachronism. The ever-increasing pressure on land space, coupled with the necessity to build high, will create a greater tendency to build underground, especially as the economics of so doing will become more and more favourable. Therefore one can certainly expect far more in the way of underground facilities such as car parks, transport interchange stations, garages, restaurants and places of entertainment.

Another factor to be taken into account will be the incorporation of VTOL airports in any major city. These will be logically incorporated on tops of buildings which will also serve as transport interchange centres between different modes of transport, from the VTOL aircraft themselves to coaches, buses and taxis down to a tube railway.'

5.12   **Alfred Wood** City Planning Officer, Norwich

'It could probably be claimed that a good deal of the current world dissatisfaction stems from environmental discontent in one form or another. Perhaps the most intractable problem is the love-hate relationship with the motor car. North America, a prosperous continent with ample land and grid-planned cities, has found itself unable to keep pace with the demand for more and more car spaces; it has become clear that a type of Parkinson's Law operates and that traffic grows to fill the road spaces available. Europe has begun to make the same discovery to its even greater cost, for with its smaller scale it has perhaps even more to lose.

Conventional traffic measures have an effect upon the appearance of a city; no-one claims that the yellow lines, the "box" junctions and the like enhance the townscape. There is little doubt that today in many towns and cities an excursion to the traffic-dominated central areas is unpleasant, frustrating and a tiring business.

It also seems that we shall be unable to redevelop our city centres on the multi-level basis considered necessary to separate vehicles and pedestrians in motorised central areas. The shortage of capital, the desire to retain historic areas and buildings of character lead me to believe that we must attempt to improve city centre conditions by environmental management measures. Foot streets can be created now in most places without major alteration to the urban fabric and with immeasurable improvement of our everyday lives.'

Motorway crossing The Lune Gorge, South from Borrowbeck.

p. 104: Traffic Congestion, Conway, Wales.

p. 104: Traffic Congestion, York.

5   Working Party Opinion

Introduction

5.13   In the planning of the human habitat the day of the supremacy of the motor car and the road-builder has come to an end. As far as public opinion is concerned this change of heart has amounted almost to a backlash. Nevertheless, the fact that the car has brought major social costs in its trail has done nothing to blunt its private popularity. Many people still find it the most comfortable, convenient and desirable means of getting about, and every other form of transport is declining.

5.14   This persistent rise in car ownership in a country which has fewer miles of road per car than anywhere else in Europe, will inevitably mean that road congestion will become a more difficult planning problem—and a major social and political issue. Road-building will continue to use a large share of our national resources, particularly at the inter-city motor-way level. But most people now realise that higher demand for road-space cannot be met indefinitely and further restraints on motor traffic will have to be introduced.

5.15   A significant sign is that congestion is no longer confined to towns and cities. In some national parks and recreation areas there is an urgent need for more car parks. Yet if a balance is not kept, this policy could be self-defeating. In Goyt Park, Derbyshire, an experimental scheme limiting public access by car and using mini-buses, may well set the pattern for other parks.

5.16   Congestion is also fast becoming a major problem in the more prosperous suburbs and country towns where car ownership and their regular use is well above the national average, and where it is impossible for adequate road-space to be provided. It is a tragedy that handsome towns such as Reigate, Warwick and Blandford, and countless small villages and suburban centres, are being torn apart by road improvement schemes which can at best be mere stop-gaps, and which may prejudice the more drastic environmental management which will have to follow in the near future. Many small towns and villages in the Home Counties are in danger of becoming intolerable places to live, work and shop, as traffic engineering tries to keep one step ahead of traffic volume.

Urban Traffic

5.17   It is in the bigger towns and cities that the conflict between traffic and the human habitat is now becoming critical. Cars, vans, lorries and coaches are important to the economic existence of towns. If town-dwellers are

prevented from keeping cars they will increasingly prefer to live in the country; if tourists cannot be transported round historic cities they will give them a miss; and perhaps most important of all, if people cannot drive to a point within easy walking distance of a particular shop or office, they will rapidly start going to shops and offices elsewhere.

5.18   There are corollaries to this which are only slowly being recognised. The out-of-town office and shopping complex so much favoured in the United States, is proving to be the surest way of killing the commercial prosperity of a city centre. The problem of rejuvenating the hearts of British provincial towns with new capital, new jobs and new attractions, is hard enough as it is without eating up the countryside round them for new shopping centres having the superficial advantage of easier vehicular access. Local authorities should look very carefully at such schemes, not merely in terms of amenity, and the likelihood of longer-term congestion, but also in terms of the impact on existing commercial centres.

By-Passes

5.19   As far as traffic in town centres is concerned, tribute should be paid to the continuing influence of Professor Colin Buchanan's great study 'Traffic in Towns', published in 1963. If it arrived too late to save some British towns from rape, there is no excuse now for others not to be saved from a similar fate. The essential thesis, which still needs continued emphasis, is that traffic which does not start or end its journey in a town should not be allowed to pass through its streets. The principle of the by-pass, long recognised in general terms, must be applied specifically and compulsorily to the central areas of every city, town, suburb and village in the country. Subordinate to that thesis is the principle that, even within such protected areas, the maximum separation of traffic and pedestrians should be achieved.

5.20   There is now, both in Britain and abroad, no shortage of examples of how these principles can be put into practice. In the case of by-passes the chief constraint is financial. The London, Manchester, Birmingham and Glasgow urban motor-way programmes—sophisticated versions of by-passes in operation—represent the greatest and most expensive public works ever undertaken by a British government in peacetime. Many people have had serious doubts about some of them, but they offer the only hope of enabling a large proportion of the population to make use of private cars to get out into the country, without making life intolerable for millions of other people.

5.21   But much more needs to be done to make primary roads less damaging to the environment through which they pass, in terms of landscaping, design and compensation. Nor do they often need to be of motorway scale—a factor which frequently postpones their starting date and thus the benefits which result from even a small relief road. In the short term, improvements can sometimes be achieved by diverting through traffic away from town centres along alternative routes which can take a larger number of vehicles. But this often means braving the ire of local residents for the sake of the wider public good.

5.22   Essential to the success of by-pass schemes, and to public acceptability of the disruption they inevitably cause, is that they can be seen to be achieving results. Nothing is more disheartening to residents looking out over a new relief road, or listening to the roar of diverted through-traffic, than to see that their local town or village is just as congested and fume-ridden as it was before. Local authorities who have summoned up the courage and the money to provide a relief road so often seem to run out of both when it comes to seeing the job through. The aim must be to prevent traffic from entering certain areas, not by sign-posting, but, ideally, by making a journey physically impossible. This is being done in countless Continental towns and villages. Why in so few in Britain?

5.23   One example of this principle is the plan for the centre of Norwich. Here the central area road pattern will eventually be based on a ring and loop system. The inner ring road, now under construction, will provide for vehicle circulation around the city centre. Penetration into the central area by private cars is to be confined to loop roads, and only buses will be allowed to use cross-centre links. This system will enable the main shopping areas and the historic areas to become virtually traffic-free during the major part of the day. Service vehicles will only be allowed access during limited periods. The main purpose of the loop roads is to provide access to car parks, whose size will be determined by the environmental capacity of the loop roads. These are mainly existing routes which in some cases will be improved. Car park capacities in the centre of the city will also be dictated by the need to avoid road widening schemes in historic streets. In this way roads and motor-vehicles are made to serve the city, rather than the city being altered to serve them.

5.24   Unfortunately, many towns have already converted their central areas to accommodate large volumes of through traffic. However, the Norwich principles can be applied in whole or in part to a wide variety of towns provided there is sufficient will on the part of planners and local politicians to carry them out. So often the deterrent to improvement is a combination of ignorance and timidity on the part of certain key local individuals.

Environmental Management

5.25   At a neighbourhood level the application of environmental management schemes is universal. Based on the same concept of confining through traffic to distributor roads, both Westminster City Council, in Pimlico, and

Islington Council, in Barnsbury, have introduced maze systems converting blocks of residential streets to a traffic pattern almost reminiscent of a rural village. Entry to the area is confined to one or two streets and no through journeys are possible. Some streets are blocked off, trees planted and variegated paving materials used. Bumps in the road known as sleeping policemen, and extended kerbs at corners called blisters, slow down neighbourhood traffic to make the streets safer for pedestrians, and parking is restricted to residents. In this way the streets can be returned to the local people.

5.26   As in the case of by-pass diversions, such schemes of environmental management can be most unpopular with residents on the roads classed as distributors. But there seems little alternative to losing amenity in certain streets for the sake of gaining it in many. There is considerable evidence that traffic on distributor roads does not increase drastically when local streets are closed off. The likelihood of increased congestion acts as a genuine deterrent to through traffic, and conditions on these roads are seldom much worse than they were before. However, roads designated as distributors must be chosen with sensitivity. There is a clear danger, with the wider extension of environmental management schemes, of their becoming twilight strips. When this happens the authorities should offer substantial rate relief along their route. There should be a clear directive from central government on this point.

Road Space

5.27   So far, we have been dealing chiefly with traffic in terms of controlling and managing the supply of road space available to it. Measures may also have to be taken to ration that space. One method is to limit it to the point of severe congestion, but this is grossly unfair to people dependent upon essential services which can only come by road—the injured and those whose houses are on fire, to name but two. Various schemes have been tested at the Road Research Laboratory which could be a financial deterrent to vehicles using certain roads, particularly in city centres. Some entail a device which is fixed to a vehicle at toll points. But this would be expensive to administer and difficult to make foolproof. Drivers have also proved notoriously insensitive to increases in the cost of motoring. Increases which penalise the hard-up motorist rather than the non-essential one are not likely to be popular or particularly advantageous.

Parking

5.28   Much the most satisfactory method of restricting the use of cars in a town has in fact proved to be controls on the freedom to park. By estimating the demand for different types of journey into town centres and by gearing parking capacity and charges accordingly, many councils have found they have a remarkably sophisticated method of controlling traffic volume and

London Street, Norwich, before pedestrianisation.

London Street, Norwich, after pedestrianisation.

direction. Others have concentrated on discouraging commuting by car where public transport is available. Some local authorities, who not so long ago were still insisting on new offices providing the maximum possible car parking space, have now turned turtle and recognised the folly of their ways. New town centre car parks should impose heavy charges on long stay parking, and few people would now defend the use of residential side streets for storing commuters' cars.

5.29   But measures to exclude through traffic and commuter traffic from town centres is not the end of the story. Commerce will die if cars, coaches or vans cannot unload people or goods within reasonable walking distance of their ultimate destination. Car parking facilities must be provided in town centres along with tolerable service access to shops and offices. Experience has shown that the best situation is a scatter of small car parks on 'loops' in from perimeter roads, their capacity geared to the likely demand for the shops and services within reach of each one. The initial charge for a short stay should be low but should rise steeply to discourage commuter parking and to increase the turnover of cars.

5.30   Vast car parks are not only unsightly but they attract traffic from all directions across the town centre. They also spell death for shops and services at a considerable distance from them. In the years to come, a carefully thought-out spread of car parking facilities round a town will be crucially important both to the quality of its environment and to the balance of its economic development. For this reason, it is impossible to over-emphasise the importance of car parking policy, including the capacity of car parks and the scale of charges, being under the strict control of the local planning authority. There is a clear need for a government direction in this matter.

Public Transport

5.31   An increased awareness of the social costs of car use in towns has led to a new resurgence of interest in public transport. In the United States, this has led to massive injections of public capital into systems which market forces had been unable to support, and which had widely been considered defunct. Public transport is now seen not merely in commercial terms but as an integral part of a mixed transport policy. It cannot entirely supplant the private car, van or lorry, in a future urban environment; in country areas, its role must become increasingly subordinate to the expanding rate of car use. But there is a risk that unnecessarily large numbers of private motor vehicles may come on the roads if public transport facilities become totally inadequate. There are important social benefits to be gained from continuing to provide public transport at a level where this tendency would be held in check. These benefits could justify subsidies from public funds in appropriate cases.

5.32   Bus services, and in the major conurbations, train services, can make the greatest contribution by transporting commuters. Park and ride schemes at London's inner suburban stations have made considerable headway. As commuting belts spread ever further they will clearly have ever wider application. Buses have experienced a catastrophic drop in total passenger mileage in Britain—from roughly a half in 1951 to a mere 14.7% today. Yet in Leeds, thirteen 'fastway' express buses have recently been introduced to link suburban areas and neighbouring communities with the central business district. The decision of the present government to introduce a freer licensing system for private bus operators, coupled with the freedom for local authorities to subsidise particular routes, should give public transport a new lease of life.

5.33   One important development in city centres, best illustrated by experience in Reading, is the introduction of bus-only lanes, often directly against the flow of traffic. These can dramatically increase the efficiency and regularity of urban transport and give it a vital competitive edge over private traffic. But the problems facing London Transport in their attempts to introduce a similar scheme in Piccadilly, show how far we still are from public acceptability for such ideas.

5.34   There are experiments to give priority to public service vehicles, including buses, in city streets closed to private traffic. At its simplest, this might be exemplified by Leeds' 'shopper's service', a mini-bus running every six, minutes through the city's precinct area. Another, as yet untried version, is the GLC's proposal for restricting traffic on the north side of Trafalgar Square. There are schemes which have been put to us for mono-rails, cab-tracks and travelators. Although some of these proposals may have a place in new environments specially designed to include them, we found that the intrusion of vehicles into pedestrian precincts is undesirable. In Germany home of the pedestrianisation concept, they are virtually unknown. Proposals for Trafalgar Square, including access for taxis, make a nonsense of any idea of a precinct.

5.35   New transport systems which either occupy permanent ground space or hurtle past overhead are likely to be no less obnoxious than the present traffic. For the vast majority of Britain's towns they could only have occasional and exceptional application. Carefully conceived roads and parking policies with good public transport for streets that are to be kept open, should minimise any inconvenience which street closures might cause to the elderly or the heavily laden.

Pedestrians

5.36   We come finally to the treatment of pedestrians—not because walking should have any lower priority, but because it is only recently that concern for the pedestrian has emerged as a dominant consideration in planning. Only a very few of the urban rebuilding projects undertaken after the war

The Southern End of Hertford Street, Coventry, before pedestrianisation.

The Southern End of Hertford Street, Coventry, after pedestrianisation.

showed much interest in pedestrianisation—Coventry was one excellent example. Since then planners and politicians have spent almost all their time and money fighting an endless, losing, guerilla warfare with traffic on wheels. Today, however, we find the Department of the Environment admitting in a recent report that 'inside every car is a pedestrian bursting to get out'. And it is a rare urban redevelopment scheme that does not pay at least some homage to planning's new-found hero.

5.37　The earliest hopes for giving pedestrians more scope in which to stretch their legs lay in schemes for traffic segregation built into new developments. Some of these have undoubtedly been successful, at least in those terms— Coventry, Cumbernauld, Basingstoke, Sheffield, to name but a few. Others may have succeeded in excluding traffic but only at the expense of visual variety, activity and convenience, and at the expense of vast sums of money into the bargain. London's Elephant and Castle and Birmingham's Bull Ring Centre are sad examples of this. However, such a principle can understandably only be applied in completely new ventures, especially where traffic, shops and pedestrians can be stacked vertically one above the other Since most town and city centres still mercifully retain the form and proportion, if not the actual buildings, of their Georgian and Victorian forebears, such concepts as vertical segregation are not easily applicable. Where they are put forward, as with the City of London's proposals for an overhead walkway right across the City area, the prospect appears simply ludicrous.

5.38　Pedestrians, on the whole, are not merely interested in walking. They want to get somewhere and do something, and they will not take kindly to planners who simply push them up to the first floor to do their walking out of harm's way—particularly when it entails ruining the appearance of many streets and buildings, spending a great deal of money and making them go a long way round as well. For this reason the chief hope must lie, in trespassing on street space at present reserved for traffic, and converting it to pedestrian use.

5.39　British experience in the pedestrianisation of existing streets is sadly extremely limited. We have yielded pride of place in this matter to countries such as Denmark and Germany, where in towns like Copenhagen, Essen and Dusseldorf, the 'foot street' movement has been well under way for some time.

5.40　It was an exciting experience to visit the traffic-free London Street in Norwich, to watch several mothers stop to have a chat while their children played without danger, and to enjoy our coffee sitting under striped umbrellas outside a cafe. The large influx in shoppers bringing a substantial increase in trade has proved the success of this experiment.

5.41   We walked down the newest foot street of all, Linthorpe Road, Middles-brough, when only a few weeks old; a caravan in the centre was full of people looking at a planning department exhibition of improvements in the surrounding area of Teesside, and there are plans for more pedestriani-sation.

5.42   An unusual feature of the foot street at Southend-on-Sea are two large and colourful kiosks with elegant canopies situated at intervals in the centre of the street. One sells fruit and flowers—the other sweets and ice-cream. Even on a cold January day we saw shoppers sitting on benches in the street to have a gossip, and the social advantages of foot streets can be a great asset to any town.

5.43   In Scotland local traders have a dramatic plan to pedestrianise Glasgow's great Sauchiehall Street sometime in 1972 in which at present traffic flows one-way in six lanes. Coventry City Council, who after the war were initiators of the pedestrian shopping precinct, have recently excluded traffic from Hertford Street, and have ambitious plans for further pedestrianisation to enhance the setting of their famous Cathedral.

5.44   The principle is the remarkably simple one of completely excluding traffic including service vans from a street, repaving it, putting in new street furniture, ensuring that goods can be delivered to stores in the street without too much inconvenience, and watching to see what happens. In the case of London Street and countless examples on the Continent, the commercial life of the street has promptly boomed and traders in other surrounding streets are crying out for similar treatment.

5.45   It is obviously important to make sure that streets closed to traffic are within easy reach of car parking facilities, and that nearby access is available for service vans. Buildings must also be accessible to emergency vehicles. The chief problem in the past has been the reluctance of local traders to believe that a customer will ever go where he cannot take his car. Resistance from traders or lethargy by local authorities has been a major problem wherever foot streets have been proposed, although the prejudices of some traffic engineers often constitute a more potent obstacle. The resistance is understandable, but patently unfounded.

5.46   All over Europe traders in streets converted from traffic routes to precincts have recorded improved turnover. The streets concerned have blossomed with renovated frontages, pavement cafes and restaurants, and have become considerable community centres in their own right. We can only hope that the widest publicity given to their success will encourage other more timid souls to follow suit.

Conclusion

5.47   In no aspect of the human habitat has public opinion and public pressure changed more radically than in transport. It has become increasingly popular to decry certain forms of transport, such as the motor car, as anti-social, without a clear understanding of its real importance to people and the needs to which they respond. These needs are real ones which cannot be wished away by those who may not share them. Nonetheless, it remains the case that the most vital requirement of modern urban planning is to find ways of taming the car before the pollution it causes and the road space it demands wipe the character and individuality off the face of countless British towns and cities.

5.48   This is not to be anti-car; it is simply to recognise that planning priorities have changed. We hope we have shown that the traffic disasters which have overtaken some British towns need not overtake all of them. We are undoubtedly behind many other countries—particularly Germany and Scandinavia—in this respect, but we still have the chance to catch up. Nothing is more important than for those who plan the future pattern of movement in our towns and cities, to be made aware of the new opportunities and alternatives which are being tried elsewhere, and are available for us to use as well.

Landscaping at Victoria Park Interchange, Glasgow.

Recommendations

22   *Local authorities should not allow town centres to be used as through roads to traffic. 'Loop' and other systems should be examined for confining through traffic to circumferential roads.*

23   *More ring roads should be developed, to allow as many streets as possible within the ring to be physically closed to through traffic.*

24   *Local authorities should examine schemes of neighbourhood environmental management for the exclusion of local through traffic from residential areas in towns and cities.*

25   *Local authorities should exercise powers to control and restrict town centre parking, since this is the most effective way of limiting car commuting.*

26   *The Government should accept the principle of public subsidy of public transport. Only if public transport undertakings receive suitable funds for development can they continue to play their part in holding down the social costs of urban congestion.*

27   *Private bus operators should be more freely licensed to provide services in deprived rural and suburban areas.*

28   *More local authorities should introduce reserved bus lanes to speed the flow of public transport.*

29   *Foot streets should be established without delay in all towns and cities.*

6 Industry and Commerce

Contents

Public Opinion   119

Working Party Opinion   125

Introduction   125

New Development   125
Industry
Commerce
Shopping

Causes of Environmental Deterioration   129
Mineral Workings
Agriculture
Energy

The Value of Environment   134

Conclusion   136

Recommendations   138

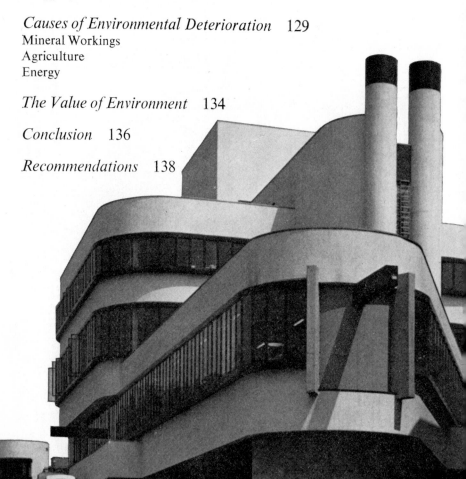

6　Public Opinion

6.1　**Professor Sir George Porter**　Director, The Royal Institution
'*Young people today, and not a few old ones, are concerned about the way the
world is going. They feel that our troubles are a result of technological
change, which, in their innocence of what science is, they identify with the
advance of science. They are doubtful about the value of material progress,
the relevance of the technology which had, until recently, been accepted as
contributing to our individual happiness and our national prosperity. Their
emphasis is the opposite of that of our Victorian grandparents; they find that
where there's brass there's muck. They accept the advantages which rapid
transport has conferred upon them but not the evils of jet noise and petrol
fumes. They accept the elimination of the terrible diseases of a few hundred
years ago as natural, but the side effects of DDT and other substances which
have eliminated those diseases as unnatural and evil. They would not wish to
face a dentist of fifty years ago but object to the use of fluoride. They are in a
grave danger of throwing out the baby with the bathwater.*'

6.2　**Royal Commission on Environmental Pollution, 1971**
'*We see no reason why a civilised society, which has already accepted the
need to provide a fair standard of living in other respects, should not now
willingly incur expenditure on the protection of its own natural environment.
Decisions in this field will reflect society's value judgement in the same way
as have decisions in many other fields of social and economic policy over the
ages. A cost-benefit analysis of the abolition of slavery might well have shown
that slavery should have been preserved; nevertheless, slavery was
abolished.*'

6.3　**H R H The Duke of Edinburgh**　Third Commonwealth Study Conference,
Australia, May/June, 1968
'*The fact is that satisfactory human communities are more important
than the industries which provide employment. People do not exist to
serve industry, it is the other way around; every industry exists for the
benefit of the people.*'

6.4　**Royal Society of Arts**
'*Industry, in the twin contexts of economic growth and the environment
as a whole, is often considered the villain of the piece. But Britain is an
industrial country which will only thrive if industry prospers—this it
can only do if it remains competitive. By the same token industry,
everywhere, has an obligation to mitigate the social consequences of*

its activities by, for example, making a substantial contribution to the cost of reducing the pollution it creates, and by making full use of derelict land for development, and diminishing its demand on land valuable in alternative uses. Therefore, in terms of building a new and more desirable environment it will clearly be necessary to reach internationally agreed criteria. We cannot impose burdens of amenity and environmental cost which Britain's industrial competitors do not bear.'

6.5 **A E Weddle** Sheffield University, writing in **'Town and Country Planning'**
'Planning authorities and industry must impose and accept as part of normal development costs the siting, design, and construction costs necessary to accommodate development acceptable to an increasingly discerning public.'

6.6 **Professor J K Page** Sheffield University
'As a physicist, I must stress the fundamental role of energy in urbanism. The first revolution was based on coal, with fuels like gas used for special purposes followed by oil and electricity generated from conventional fuels. The next energy revolution will be based upon nuclear power. The problems of pollution of towns in the UK have been traditionally associated with the combustion of coal with its problems of smoke, sulphur dioxide, grit and ash. On present trends domestic coal consumption could fall from twenty four million tons in 1967 to 3½ million tons in the year 2000. The environmental consequences of this change will be important.
The availability of this cheap and easily controllable amount of electrical energy will have enormous implications for environmental engineering, because it will become possible to maintain relatively large areas of towns in inhospitable climates at attractive levels of comfort.
The incipient signs of all these changes have been present in some recent international exhibitions, especially Montreal, but by the year 2,000, towns like Wigan, Bootle and Halifax will not only have clean air but will have the capacity to create recreational spaces used in winter that could be the environmental equivalent of the Bahamas or Barbados.'

6.7 **The British Mountaineering Council**
'We are concerned at the establishment of industries, excluding of course agriculture, in mountain country, which involve more roads and buildings which may not be in keeping with the landscape. The installation of further hydro-power works as is now proposed in North Wales, is a typical example. It is appreciated that hydro-electric schemes are only possible in mountain country, but these should be limited, and where acceptable, blended into the countryside.'

6.8 **National Council of Women of Great Britain**
*'We must not forget that the demand for land increases from year to year.
John Taylor, of the Associated Portland Cement Manufacturers, estimated
that by 1980 a further 172,500 acres of gravel bearing land will be needed.
By 1972, twelve new nuclear power stations will have swallowed up 6,000
acres. Every airport for Jumbo Jets, with its ancillary buildings, eats up
10,000 acres, and even a humble oil refinery or sea gas terminal calls for
1,000 and 2,000 acres respectively.'*

6.9 **The Horsham Society** Sussex
*'In common with the tendency to regard land as inexhaustible, there is also a
tendency to regard the countryside as a playground and to forget that it is
also an industry.'*

6.10 **The Ramblers Association**
*'We cannot see why farmers should be exempt from the full rigour of
planning control of new buildings. Mass-produced, cheap and often shoddy
working farm structures are readily available today and demand a measure
of control which was perhaps less necessary when a building required more
time, more care, and more attention to detail.'*

6.11 **Crown Estate Commissioners**
*'We are always concerned that new farm buildings should be sited and
designed to fit into the landscape, and are very ready to bear additional costs
which may be involved in this, including the cost of coloured sheeting which is
being used increasingly instead of stark asbestos.'*

6.12 **The Scottish Landowners Federation**
*'Modern pressures and economics force farmers to remove hedgerows, cut
down trees and clear unproductive shrub areas. The maintenance of a
proportion of these features from an environment and ecological angle is very
important. We consider that rather than a hedgerow grubbing grant, there
should be some incentive to maintain these features.'*

6.13 **The Director** February 1970, Journal of the Institute of Directors
*'Many of the improvements in Britain's amenities over recent years have
arisen from carefully planned industrial expansion. Industrialists are fully
aware of their social obligations, and clean and attractive factories are more
efficient and more attractive places for both managers and work-people.'*

6.14 **British Steel Corporation**
*'It is a sad situation that despite efforts from many sources, the area of
dereliction in Great Britain continues to grow and that indications are that
this rate is likely to increase rather than decrease.
Industry in the past, has much to answer for the dereliction of land. However,*

in the past decade or more, there has been a significant change to a positive policy within the iron and steel industry to eliminate, as far as possible, the creation of derelict land, and a policy to remove blemishes which have been created in the past. We fully recognise our responsibility in this matter and realise that this policy means a considerable expense to our industry. We accept this as a right and proper expenditure. Under present legislation, only derelict land which is owned by a local authority attracts an 85% central government grant towards the costs of remedial landscape measures. The owner or industrial undertaking receives no support for any work he does within his own boundaries. This can act as a deterrent to speedy action and to research into amelioration techniques. Many of the worst eyesores are the result of neglect by third parties many years ago.'

6.15 **Civic Trust for the North West**

'In a region which is still suffering the ravages of the Industrial Revolution, and has consistently failed to attract new industry, and suffers an annual migration out of the region, it is easy to show a correlation between a poor environment, economic stagnation and unemployment. Such government incentives as have been used in the region have always been related to unemployment and channelled through such devices as Development Districts and Intermediate Areas, when a more lasting contribution to economic vitality and full employment might have been achieved by directing such finances to the areas of the greatest environmental need.'

The Welsh Glass Works, Swansea, Wales.

Yardley Factory, Basildon.

6 Working Party Opinion

Introduction

6.16 Britain is an industrial country and will only thrive if we maintain a prosperous economy. This has been the recurring theme that has been stressed by all governments since the last war. The magic word—growth. It appears to be an article of faith that all our ills, whether physical, social or economic, can be cured if only we can achieve ever higher rates of growth. Consequently, economic development with its massive demands upon our resources, has received priority whether or not the environment could withstand the onslaught. At the same time, the majority of people have demanded a higher standard of living. Thus we are all responsible for this headlong drive for growth, and the consequential chain of resources —production—consumption.

6.17 It is only recently that we have realised that there is also an environmental price to be paid for the products of this economic drive. Huge sections of industry are now moving into much more environmentally destructive patterns of production. This is positively encouraged when we measure growth in terms of purely economic gain and leave out any assessment of environmental losses. The result is a growth which can only be described as a Rake's Progress.

6.18 The urban environment is where industry and commerce are created. It should also be where the quality of life improves. But when a private developer is building a factory or a shopping centre, or a public developer is building a power station or a hospital, environmental considerations are too often viewed as merely on-costs which could place the whole project in jeopardy. These economic concepts are those evolved by society itself. If the resulting environment is unacceptable, it must be pointed out that we get what we pay for.

New Development

Industry

6.19 If a beautiful stretch of coastline is sacrificed to the building of an oil refinery, it is not because that refinery could not be developed a few miles inland on some less environmentally important site, it is because the capital cost of the project might increase by ten per cent. That extra cost would have to be reflected in the cost of the petrol and oil produced, and ultimately in the cost of transporting the commodities we buy.

Portsmouth Building Society Offices. Civic Trust Award 1969.
p. 128 St Helen's Office Building, London. Civic Trust Award 1970.
below: Cockenzie Power Station, Scotland. Civic Trust Award.

6.20 It is the same story with the development of steel foundries, petro-chemical complexes or aluminium works, all of which are growing in size and number. Recent studies have shown that the rate of growth in these basic industries is of the order of 10% per annum. Vast capital investments must be committed in new plant, where the prime objective will be to achieve the economies which flow from increasing scale and continuous methods of production. These particular industries are often inter-dependent for supplies, and as a result there is a distinct tendency for them to agglomerate. Consequently these new industrial monsters defy visual containment, demand an extensive and complex infrastructure, and concentrate pollution hazards. Another problem is that they are typical of the new generation of economic development which is often multi-national in composition and trades on an international basis. For this reason we cannot impose upon them heavy extra costs to protect amenity which Britain's industrial competitors do not face, without running a grave risk to our whole economy.

Commerce

6.21 Office employment is perhaps our fastest growing industry. Pressure for more office floor space in the centre of towns, higher land values due to the scarcity of good sites, and industrialised building techniques have resulted in an ever-increasing scale and density of commercial development. At the same time, rising costs are reducing the design of these office complexes to simple standard forms.

6.22 Environmental consequences, human scale, street scene, skyline, and the generation of traffic, are matters which are subordinated to economic viability. That is not to say that these factors are never considered; they usually are, but seldom, if ever, on equal terms. More often than not they are the first items to be sacrificed if the required percentage return on investment cannot be realised. The developer can legitimately point to the fact that he is caught up in a system which demands this market approach. If he does not produce a solution which realises the necessary economic return, the proposed investment will merely be transferred to an alternative outlet or to another developer.

Shopping

6.23 Over the last few years modern trends in retail distribution have resulted in increasing pressure for out of town shopping centres. The growing demands of departmental and chain stores for ground floor sales space and storage, the emergence of larger supermarkets and discount stores, have meant that these cannot always be accommodated in the traditional High Street. In addition, increasing traffic congestion, and lack of parking and servicing facilities, have driven developers to seek alternative solutions.

6.24   The most significant influence upon shopping habits is the motor car, and in the Traffic section of our Report we discuss the need to provide adequate transport facilities which will allow the creation of foot streets. This is vital if our town centres are to prosper. To ensure this, there are perhaps even more fundamental policy considerations which must be resolved.

6.25   The continuing exodus from city centres will inevitably result in a reduction there in the demand for consumer goods. This will be accompanied by a growth of suburban shopping centres in any new residential districts. Associated with this natural outward movement there are pressures to extend these new centres for trading in durables. Meantime, out-of-town shopping centres and huge hyper-markets threaten the basis of existing retail distribution.

6.26   Town centres are much more than a collection of shops. They are the heart of an area. From time immemorial civic life, culture, entertainment, recreation and the interchange of opinion have taken place in town centres. Early cities were built round the Greek 'agora' or the Roman 'forum'. The 'piazza', the 'place', the 'plaza', usually dominated by the town hall or the church, are a feature of towns and cities all over Europe. There are often in the vicinity many buildings of great historic or architectural value.

6.27   Today in Britain the over-powering effect of traffic on both people and buildings must be lessened to enable our town centres to have a viable future, and to permit a far higher standard of environment. Before this can be achieved there should be no question of allowing the development of massive out-of-town shopping facilities. Traditional town centres would as a result be stripped of their important retail functions and their vitality destroyed. The economic and environmental depression would kill them.

6.28   But local authorities should realise that in order to resist demands for out of town shopping centres they must make their central shopping areas more convenient and more attractive places in which customers can spend their money. The removal of traffic is essential, coupled with the provision of adjacent car parks and efficient public transport nearby.

Causes of Environmental Deterioration

6.29   We have so far referred to the more obvious fields of industrial and commercial change. The increasing pace and scale of this change has caused throughout the country a profound unease at the destructive effects of growth and development. There is also a growing distrust of policies which provide for increased economic well-being while neglecting environmental safeguards. The process of industrialisation usually accompanies urbanisation, but environmental deterioration can be attributed more directly to industrialisation.

6.30   There are specific problems related to the development of essential industries. The location of cement works, brickworks, metallurgical industries, coal mines or power plants are largely dictated by the presence of minerals, power or water. Undertakings which involve the construction of large-scale dams, reservoirs, canals, power stations, transmission lines and other visually dominant structures are of particular concern. Reference has already been made to the increasing scale of the industrial plants themselves and the tendency to agglomerate. Pollution problems are superimposed upon all these physical aspects compounding the total environmental dilemma.

Mineral Workings

6.31   Roads, airports, or other buildings require increasing quantities of gravel, cement and raw materials. To deal with our industrial needs huge mineral excavations are anticipated. The areas of search for deposits must, for economic reasons, be as close to the centres of demand as nature allows. This means that the visual scars created by the mining of these materials will occur in the countryside near to urban areas. This is usually where there is the greatest need of land for agriculture and recreation. Mineral undertakers have to make plans a long way ahead, since heavy initial capital expenditure is often involved, so they need to be sure that extraction opportunities will be available well into the future. The working life of a quarry of up to fifty years is not uncommon, while planning periods in excess of that can apply in respect of certain deposits. This scale and duration of working mineral deposits can produce a running sore in the local environment. It is essential that restoration or landscaping should be done concurrently. To achieve this it may be necessary to consider imposing upon the industry the full social costs of the damage they cause. This would include the elimination of waste, and the collection, treatment and removal of unwanted by-products of the process.

6.32   In some areas much has already been achieved and the changing pattern of industry will ensure that in the future we are unlikely to see the gigantic waste tips and dereliction similar to those left from the first industrial revolution. Some local authorities are making massive efforts to clear and reclaim inherited areas of dereliction, but the sheer scale of operation when hundreds of thousands of acres are involved requires more drastic action.

6.33   One of the problems is that often the worst areas are those which also suffer from economic stagnation, and despite the grants available they are least able to cope with the task of rehabilitation. Another difficulty is that under present legislation, only derelict land which is owned by local authorities attracts grants for reclamation. Private owners or industrial undertakings receive nothing. Yet owners long since dead, or third parties who have now disappeared, caused a great deal of damage for which present owners cannot be held responsible. The Government should take urgent steps to solve this particular aspect of the problem.

Agriculture

6.34 Agriculture as an industry is also subject to modern economic pressures, which force farmers to remove hedgerows, cut down trees, clear unproductive shrub areas, mechanise their cultivation methods, and industrialise their breeding and production techniques. To help them in these objectives grants are often available. It could be argued that in order to maintain a balance from the ecological and environmental points of view the reverse should apply. But as urbanisation continues to make extensive demands upon agricultural land, as motorways develop and disturb agricultural units, as the mining of raw materials takes land even temporarily out of production, then more food from an ever-reducing quantity of agricultural land is a goal which we must support. Consequently, industrialised techniques in farming are essential.

6.35 There have been a considerable number of complaints from our contributors that agricultural buildings are at present outside the planning laws. The siting, materials, and design of the majority leave much to be desired, yet it would be laughable to force a farmer to build a milking parlour or a covered yard in an inconvenient place for his livestock simply because it then looked more attractive. However, materials such as stark white asbestos are visually obtrusive and many farm buildings are unnecessarily ugly. We would like to see co-operation between the National Farmers Union and the Department of the Environment to work out a form of planning control for farm buildings which would be acceptable to farmers and to the general public.

Energy

6.36 We live in an energy-hungry era. The first industrial revolution was based on coal, with fuels like gas for special purposes, followed by oil and electricity generated from conventional fuels. The recent exploitation of natural gas followed, but the next energy revolution will be based upon nuclear power. This should help to overcome many of the problems of urban pollution which result from the emission of smoke, sulphur dioxide, grit and ash.

6.37 Unfortunately, the technology of transmission of electrical power has not kept pace with the advances in generating that power. Transmission capacity has improved, but the technique of overhead power lines suspended from large towers which march so aggressively across the landscape in ever growing numbers, is surely a method which must be replaced if our relatively small island is not eventually to resemble a space-scale cobweb.

6.38 The application of our nuclear technology appears to be directed towards the creation of ever larger power stations. These must be sited on the coast because they require vast quantities of cooling water. From these locations radiate the transmission grids to serve the centres of demand. We would

benefit by a policy of developing small nuclear stations nearer to thos centres. The smaller stations could be blended into the landscape, man transmission lines could be eliminated, and at least one pressure upon th coastline removed.

6.39 Nowadays large quantities of energy and other materials have to b transported over long distances. This improves the possibility of usin underground pipelines. Pipelines progressively become more viable a volume and distance increase, especially when used to transport ra materials such as oil, chemicals and coal, or commodities like garbage an industrial waste. In recent years natural gas and crude oil pipelines hav been developed in Britain, but little has been done to develop technique for conveying other materials and products. The extensive pipeline net works being created on the continent, planning techniques such as th 'pipeline streets' in the Netherlands, are all advances which should b carefully studied to see if they could help our particular problem.

6.40 The ever growing numbers of oil storage tanks are another environmenta hazard. Pipeline studies should be extended to incorporate undergroun techniques for the bulk storage of oil. Rock tunnels or caverns create below ground would reduce the demand on land, and contamination pollution, and fire hazards would be greatly diminished.

The Value of Environment

6.41 The quality of the environment is an important factor in the industrial attraction of an area, and is certainly taken into account by any industrialist when considering the establishment of a new plant. There is an obvious link between a poor environment, economic depression, unemployment, and outward migration. National policies which offer inducements to industrialists to locate new factories in such areas could be justified on social grounds alone.

6.42 However, there is a complementary need for positive environmental improvement. Only when these twin objectives, social and environmental, find a place in our policies, will they be truly effective in creating economic prosperity in what are usually classified as depressed areas. The benefits of efficiency are undeniable, and the potential of technological power is enormous. But as economic productivity increases, so will the exploitation of resources, and the physical disruption of the environment. This could result in a great concentration of urban conurbations and the massive erosion of the countryside.

pp. 132, 133: Fincham Hall Barn, Norfolk.

opposite: Gas Works, Llandarcy, Glamorgan. RIBA Regional Award 1966.

Conclusion

6.43　In order to find the right balance between conflicting economic an[d] environmental factors, there will need to be a shift from predominant[ly] financial and technical criteria, to social and human criteria, for every kin[d] of new development. We must stop abusing our environment and us[e] some of our technical tools for environmental advancement. We shoul[d] study the negative effects of our economic and technical policies, just as w[e] study the positive aspects. At the same time, we cannot afford to price ou[r] products out of world markets by imposing prohibitive costs upon ou[r] industries.

6.44　Among industrialists as a whole, we found an increased awareness of th[e] necessity to protect and enhance the environment. Not only finance i[s] necessary. More thought is required to prevent haphazard siting of ne[w] industries; more instant landscaping and tree planting is required to scree[n] industrial plant; there should be better designs for new factories, an[d] every effort made to minimise land requirements. The first step is to tak[e] our heads out of the sand and to see clearly the dangers ahead. If tech[-]nology can enable man to land on the moon, surely it can help him to solv[e] the problems which are on his own doorstep?

below: Raschel Knitting Factory, Swansea. Civic Trust Award.

opposite: Kodak Building, Hemel Hempstead.

Recommendations

30   *Because of the growing scale of industrial plant and th tendency to agglomerate, the cumulative effect should b anticipated by assessing the environmental capacity of an are to absorb them.*

31   *With so many major industrial installations gravitating to th coast and towards deep water facilities, a policy of develop ment inland from these points should be adopted wheneve possible, rather than to allow industrial growth to proliferat along the coastline.*

32   *In areas of commercial pressure the capacity of the area t contain massive increases in office floor space should be mor strictly assessed, with a greater emphasis on the environmenta consequences.*

33   *While recognising the need for changes in the structure o retailing, major out-of-town shopping centres or hyper-market should only be allowed in exceptional cases and where n damage to existing nearby town centres would result.*

34   *There should be a faster rehabilitation of inherited areas o dereliction, more assistance to local authorities whose area have suffered economic decline as a result, and grants fo rehabilitation of derelict land in private or in industria ownership.*

35   *The National Farmers Union and the Department of th Environment should co-operate to draw up a form of planning control for farm buildings.*

36   *We recommend greater research be undertaken into energy transmission methods and transportation of products, with particular reference to the transmission of electrical power and underground pipelines.*

37   *In economic policies towards depressed areas, greater effort should be made to achieve positive environmental improve ments.*

38   *There should be a general shift of emphasis from predominantly economic and technical, to social and human criteria, for new development of all kinds.*

7 Recreation

Contents

Public Opinion   141

Working Party Opinion   147

Introduction   147

Recreation in Towns and Cities   147
Parks
Leisure Centres
Museums
Cultural Activities
Walks
Canals

Recreation in the Country   158
Parks
Caravans
Camping
Open-Air Museums

Tourism   162

Conclusion   162

Recommendations   166

7 Public Opinion

7.1 Ralph Dutton Extract from 'The English Country House'

'*No nation has the love of country life more firmly implanted in its character than the English, and it is an unfortunate chance that few, if any, European countries possess a larger proportion of urban population. This apparent inconsistency is accounted for by economic needs, still, it seems in process of fulfilment—a process that is gradually depleting the countryside of its population and swelling the towns to unwieldy and frightening proportions.*'

7.2 Taken for Granted Report of the Working Party on Sewage Disposal— 1970

'*As more people own cars and enjoy longer hours of leisure, there has recently been a great increase in outdoor recreation. Its most popular form is taking a trip in the car with the family to some place of interest, which is often by a river or stretch of water. Angling has increased by 50% between 1954 and 1964. In 1966 there were estimated to be three million anglers, more people than participated in any other sport except swimming. Boating is thought to have increased twelve-fold between 1952 and 1962 and the number of boatmen was estimated to be 700,000 in 1966 (50,000 less than golfers but 50,000 more than amateur football players). In 1965 there were 5 boats to every 1,000 people. There were in 1966 about 45,000 rowers and 35,000 canoers. Water skiers have increased from a handful in 1955 to over 75,000 in 1966.*'

7.3 St Agnes Amenity Society Cornwall

'*What we in this Society are pledged to oppose is the prostitution of our rural areas to mass entertainment, with all that such prostitution would involve; including the defilement of the natural landscape, the pollution of the atmosphere and the infliction of noise on an otherwise peaceful area.*'

7.4 The Petersfield Society Hampshire

'*Certain rural areas should be reserved for recreation, as is now being done in the creation of country parks. But it is important that this should not be done where there is a countryside and flora and fauna of special interest. Such areas are destroyed by sheer numbers of people, and the damage is made worse by those who misuse the land. Such areas should not be given publicity.*'

7.5 **David Wiggins** Bedford College, London

'The railways still have a great recreational function to perform. The old cry "everyone has a car these days" is at best still only half a truth. The census return of 1966 showed that 56% of households lacked use of a car, a figure which has presumably declined only a few percentage points since. It follows that millions of people are dependent on public transport—and the railways especially—for a day by the sea, a walk in the country or an annual holiday. If they were not, the pressure on some areas of scenic beauty would already be intolerable. What such people need is cross-country or rural rail services and stations or halts in open country. Any local consortium, group or council should have first refusal, before closure is effected, to take over the line and its fixed assets from British Rail.'

7.6 **Tomorrow's Glasgow** University of Strathclyde, Glasgow

'One of the immediate objectives is to link up many of the existing open spaces to create parkland trunk routes using the courses of rivers and canals and disused railways.'

7.7 **Ben Whitaker and Kenneth Browne** Extract from **'Parks for People'**

'Mid-town greenery is needed for office-workers and shoppers within walking range during their lunch breaks.'

7.8 **Professor Page** Sheffield University Extract from **'Biology and the Future of Man'** 1971

'The games of the future may well have to be different from the past, simply because traditional games use so much land. But one must remind oneself that the palace courtyard of Henry V of France produced tennis: the steps of Eton College Chapel, fives; Deans Yard, Westminster, football. At least some of the modern games come from an urban mould. Perhaps we will see a re-adoption of the concept of urban games in our society, now pressures on land are severe.'

7.9 **Council for the Protection of Rural England** Hampshire

'I think galleries, concert halls, museums and theatres extremely important. I think it would be useful to have some paying days and some free. People often value more what they pay for.'

7.10 **The Woodley and Earley Society** Berkshire

'Art galleries, or concert halls are obviously of great importance, but one wonders if the days of the purpose-built gallery have passed. Parts of public buildings or community centres should be given over to either permanent exhibition centres or centres where exhibitions could be held at regular intervals. All community centres should be built with a hall which could be used as a concert hall.'

7.11   **The Theatrical Management Association**
        *'There can be no doubt that a theatre is a benefit to a community, and we can
        be very proud that, despite enormous obstacles, there is still so much live
        entertainment of all sorts being offered in England today, and that the
        standard is generally so high. At the moment the provincial theatre is in the
        process of rebirth. There are only thirty or so commercial theatres left in the
        provinces, but the municipal theatres are expanding and improving, with the
        help of the ratepayers, and the Arts Council, and the standard of entertain-
        ment is often as high as the standard to be seen in the West End of London.*

7.12   **British Tourist Authority**
        *'Tourism can provide a new economic resource, particularly in areas which
        are lacking in industrial development. Cultural activities can exist which
        could not be supported by local interest alone—the most obvious example of
        this is in London where overseas visitors provide about 50% of all theatre
        attendances.'*

7.13   **Chelmsford Society** Essex
        *'It is questionable whether too many facilities for car-parking picnicking, etc,
        should be provided, lest the beauty spot should become too popular and too
        much used, thus losing its quiet charm, for example, parts of the Lake
        District.'*

7.14   **Stafford Historical and Civic Society**
        *'Greater control of the ever increasing number of caravans is called for, as the
        proliferation of these either on permanent sites or towed hither and thither
        presents one of the greatest threats to the peace and serenity of our coast
        and countryside. A minority view suggests that the government might well
        consider the imposition of a significant tax on caravans.'*

7.15   **Friends of the Lake District** Westmorland (Newsletter January 1971)
        *'We have written on many occasions in past years about the need for strict
        planning control on a new caravan site, and the importance of allowing none
        on lake shores. We have, however, also contended that, if suitably painted,
        caravans would make less impact on the countryside than they now do, and
        we note that during the past year the Planning Board has for the first time
        imposed a condition regarding colour when granting an application. This
        concerned a site in the Vale of Lorton and provided that all caravans
        remaining for a period in excess of twenty one days, "shall be painted in one
        or more dark colours to the satisfaction of the Local Planning Authority".*

7.16   **The Ramblers Association**
        *'There are just over 100,000 miles of public footpaths and bridleways
        criss-crossing the English and Welsh countryside, a priceless recreational
        asset and a unique one. But the paths are continually threatened. It is the*

stated policy of the National Farmers Union to "rationalise" the paths, by which they mean to reduce drastically the total mileage. Nearly 500 paths are legally extinguished every year, and of the remainder all too few are signposted and many are ploughed up, overgrown or otherwise illegally obstructed. The sums required to signpost them adequately, to keep them clear of overgrowth, to check them for obstructions and other infringements and to maintain gates, stiles and bridges along them are relatively insignificant.'

7.17   **British Cycling Bureau**
'The British Cycling Bureau will petition for special paths, which will segregate cyclists from motor traffic, thus not only reducing traffic congestion but also giving greater road safety to cyclists. Town planners will be persuaded to include cycle ways as part of civic planning. The campaign will also negotiate for better recreational facilities in public parks and on land owned by the Forestry Commission.'

7.18   **The Institute of Housing Managers** Miss Cockburn, Housing Manager of Bracknell Development Corporation
'People need an object for an expedition; for example, a Safari Park, a point-to-point, the river, the sea, the downs or mountains. These desires must be catered for and it is no good thinking that the countryside will provide recreation if it is entirely barbed-wired with "private", "keep out", "no footpath", "no parking", notices everywhere.'

7.19   **Diana Fawkes** Winchester, Hants
'Hampshire over the last few years or so have organised a variety of public open spaces throughout the country in an attempt to provide easily accessible recreation areas, and to reduce the pressure on the coast and the New Forest.'

7.20   **Ulster Farmers' Union**
'Legislation exists in Northern Ireland under which a Government department can designate an area as one of "outstanding natural beauty". The effect of such designations can be to attract more visitors to the area than the available amenities can cope with, thus destroying their attraction for those who enjoyed these areas. Even if local authorities had finance to provide facilities such as better roads, parking places, or recreational areas, it is doubtful, whether such developments make the area more attractive to those who considered it beautiful originally.'

7.21   **The Countryside in 1970** Extract
'At the beginning of 1969 the National Trust held an area of land amounting to one per cent of the total land area of England and Wales. They have provided new car parks, camping sites, caravan sites, information centres,

lavatories, picnic sites and facilities for refreshments on many of their public open spaces, and have often been assisted in this by local authorities. They have also constructed nature trails and new footpaths on many of their properties.'

7.22 **The Inland Waterways Association** John Humphries, Chairman
'In England we have inherited a network of 2,000 miles of waterways which pass through the most glorious unspoilt countryside and which intersect almost every major industrial conurbation. It is not generally know that there are more miles of canal in the Birmingham area than there are in Venice.'

7.23 **Association of River Authorities**
'Rivers in particular, perhaps more than coast-line or lakes, must be recognised as part of the everyday setting for living and working. There need to be places in towns as well as in the country where the occasional angler may quietly and hopefully dangle his line.'

7.24 **Metropolitan Water Board**
'The Board's prime responsibility is to supply adequate quantities of wholesome water to six million people, who far outnumber those who might ultimately participate in water-based leisure activities on the Board's reservoirs.

7.25 **A M Edwards and G P Wibberley** Extract from **'An Agricultural Land Budget for Britain—1965-2000'**
'The ability of the individual to take part in recreational activities is conditioned by the length of the working week and the length of the annual holiday, and by the size of personal income. In addition the level of education attained, and the degree of personal mobility are important. In the United Kingdom all these factors are moving in a positive direction to increase the demand for outdoor recreation. This has important implications for rural land use, since the basic resource required for many forms of recreation is land. Urban sports centres and inland waterways will be important but areas of land in the countryside will also be wanted.'

7   Working Party Opinion

Introduction

7.26   Recreation and leisure are becoming more and more sophisticated. People do not just want an outing. They want something to do when they get there, and they require a higher standard of comfort. Elaborately equipped caravans have rapidly increasing sales, and so have folding tables, chairs and sun umbrellas for picnics. Another trend, seemingly in conflict, is a back-to-nature movement by those who want to be alone; to watch wildlife or to walk over fields free from their fellow human beings. The countryside is thus in demand more than ever for three uses: organised recreation, unorganised recreation, and for the industry of agriculture which provides nearly half the food eaten by the population of Great Britain. But the majority of people live in towns and do not always have the time or the transport to go very far afield, so that new facilities for urban recreation are vital.

Recreation in Towns and Cities

Parks

7.27   The traditional place for recreation has always been the parks, and there are surprisingly beautiful parks in the centre of many towns and cities, often donated to the borough by a Victorian industrialist, or bought by the local authority from a large landowner, when death duties or an expanding population drove him away from his country seat, which became unexpectedly part of the town. These parks are both an aesthetic and financial asset. Albert Park in Middlesbrough not only provides one hundred acres of greenery near the town centre, but is well laid out with tennis courts and boating facilities. The central feature of the lovely park at Stoke-on-Trent, Staffordshire, is an Edwardian bandstand with wrought-iron railings, and the ground is terraced down to a lake where swans glide to and fro. Below a bridge is the canal, and there are plans to open this for water recreation, which would link up with work done by voluntary labour to clear stretches of the Caldon Canal a few miles upstream.

7.28   When we visited Ropner Park at Stockton-on-Tees in October, the flowers were still lovely, but it is the Corporation of Brighton, Sussex, who deserve first prize for the gorgeous variety of flowers and shrubs in all their parks. The network of parks in London can best be understood when circling in an aeroplane before landing at Heathrow. Many visitors are surprised to

The Maltings Concert Hall, Snape, Suffolk. Civic Trust Award 1968.

147

The River Thames at Corporation Park, near Reading Bridge.

find that they can walk for miles from Whitehall to Kensington with only a few roads to cross, via St James Park, Green Park, Hyde Park, Kensington Gardens and Holland Park. Some parks or commons, however, are frankly depressing, and need a new look; they are unkempt and neglected have few amenities and a general air of 'keep off the grass'.

7.29 Parks are not always situated near enough for workers to get the benefit during their lunch hour, and we feel it is essential to provide small gardens in built-up areas. There are over ninety in the City of London, some of which were initiated by the Metropolitan Public Gardens Association, and which are now cared for by the Corporation. Some are tiny—but even a couple of seats and a few shrubs may be a welcome oasis to secretaries or shoppers. Coventry City Council have plans to link Swanswell Park and Lady Herbert's garden beneath the arches of the elevated Ring Road, and we think that many other towns should make a positive effort to provide these much-needed environmental areas. In Glasgow, there is a scheme to link existing parks with new 'walkways'. Disused railway lines leading from Victoria Park have been used to create the Victoria Walkway already green and attractive after only a few years by the planting of semi-mature trees and shrubs. A long-term plan for further green fingers of this kind will result in walkways right through to Loch Lomond.

Leisure Centres

7.30   A more elaborate form of town recreation is the purpose-built Leisure or Sports Centre. The Forum in Billingham has one and a quarter million people through the turnstiles every year. Swimming, ice-skating and going to the well-equipped theatre are the most popular activities, but air-rifle shooting, archery and squash, besides many other facilities are available on the two acre site. Basingstoke Sports Centre, built by private subscriptions and public funds, is right in the pedestrian shopping precinct and has a restaurant which overlooks Porchester Square. Special equipment enables spastics and cripples to use the swimming pool. A creche with an organised play group is available for children, while mothers can attend yoga classes or fathers do weightlifting. The main hall which seats 1,200 is a venue for concerts, dances or wrestling, while other rooms, all with excellent lighting, are marked out for squash, tennis and badminton.

Theatre at the Forum, Billingham.

overpage: The Theatre Royal, York.

7.31 The Pavilion at Thornaby specialises in do-it-yourself, and has a sma staff. The indoor bowls club is an important feature, and voluntee organise amateur dramatics, keep-fit classes or poetry reading. Meado bank, Edinburgh, was built for the Commonwealth Games. It has stadium with all weather 'Tartan' track, but facilities for indoor ba minton, swimming, table tennis and five-a-side football are available f members and established sports clubs. In London the Crystal Pala Centre has a championship swimming pool and a dry ski-slope, while Cardiff, the National Sports centre for Wales, among many excelle facilities, features a lecture theatre, to seat 100, and 36 double and sing bedrooms for members of visiting sports clubs. There is no doubt th sport and leisure centres have been a great success, and the fact th people are prepared to pay for their enjoyment and in some cases enr for family membership, proves a need for this particular form of leisu outlet which can be used in both winter and summer.

The Dry Ski Slope, Crystal Palace, London.

Toy Display, Bethnal Green Museum.

Museums

7.32   For those who are not so energetic, museums can be a great interest. In the last ten years attendances have gone up by 80%. But some are gloomy and old-fashioned, and need a lighter touch. In contrast, the Castle Museum at York, which attracts 750,000 visitors a year, is nearly always full of children obviously enjoying themselves. The replicas of an eighteenth century sweet shop and a post office with bay windows, the cobbled street with a horse-drawn carriage, are far more educational than many hours spent poring over history books. The museum at Preston Hall, Stockton, has period rooms complete in every detail, such as a miner's parlour, and a Victorian nursery, and they are now creating period streets. The Geffrye Museum, housed in former seventeenth century alms-houses at Shoreditch, has a series of rooms throughout the ages right up to the present day.

7.33   Bethnal Green Museum, London, has a fascinating collection of clothes, dolls, dollshouses, art nouveau glass, furniture and objects of the nineteenth century. An outstanding feature is the Italian Marionette Theatre, and during the school holidays there is an Education Officer to teach puppet-making, mural painting, or to tell stories relating to the treasures of the museum. This is a brilliant idea and highly successful. The new Army

Museum in Chelsea offers visitors a panorama of British Military history from 1485 to 1914. Famous sieges, battles, or entire wars are explained on easily read panels. Uniforms, swords and medals are shown against a background of brilliantly coloured felts, and push-button music ranged from 'The British Grenadiers', to 'Goodbye Dolly Gray'.

7.34   In the long-established Victoria and Albert Museum in Kensington, the Jones collection of French furniture and continental porcelain, has been re-arranged with great imagination. This museum has a special department which caters for their seventy five travelling exhibitions, ranging from important Indian sculpture, to drawings of Winnie the Pooh, to be shown in local museums all over England. Considerable material also goes to schools and training colleges. There are ideas to extend this so that exhibitions could also be seen in public libraries. Funds should be available so that this successful scheme could be copied by other National museums and galleries where all too often storerooms are packed with pictures objects which may never reach the public.

7.35   Temporary exhibitions with unusual themes, such as the 'Victorian Way Death' at the Brighton Art Gallery, or 'Samuel Pepys Esq' at the National Portrait Gallery, have proved that they draw in the crowds. So did the exquisitely arranged 'Orange and the Rose' at the Victoria and Albert and the dramatic 'Elizabethan Image' at the Tate. Once having enjoyed themselves, visitors may return to see the permanent collection.

7.36   But older museums need more comforts such as seats and fitted carpets. Lighting should be more subtle. Restaurants or cafes should be attached. In many places a far more interesting artistic arrangement would vastly improve the setting of the unequalled collection of pictures, furniture and other works of art which are available for the public to admire in Great Britain. We are also in favour of an idea put forward by Dr Roy Strong that museums and galleries should be more flexible in their opening times. It would be most exciting if they could become part of an evening entertainment, like films, concerts, or the theatre, instead of shutting the doors at five or six pm, just when the majority of people are free.

Cultural Activities

7.37   We were most impressed by the Report of the Arts Council on their activities, and heard praise of their work from all sides. In 1969-70 the grants to help every kind of cultural endeavour, financed by the Government, totalled over £8 million. An important suggestion was made by several of our contributors that concert halls, galleries or theatres should be multi-purpose. When redevelopment takes place in towns, older halls are often swept away, and not replaced, and this has also caused a dearth of meeting places for amateur artistic groups of all kinds. Redundant

Roberts' Display Case Story of the Army Exhibition. National Army Museum.

churches, if in reasonable condition, and if they could be altered an properly heated, might provide new premises for arts centres.

7.38   We were full of admiration for the work in Haddington, Scotland, of th Lamp of Lothian Collegiate Trust, where a youth club, experiment: music and theatre for young people, pottery, painting, and a literar society, have all been promoted on a voluntary basis, and members use group of converted historic buildings for their many artistic activitie This whole concept is one which should be copied in many other area

Walks

7.39   There are those who sometimes feel they want to get away from crowc and go for a quiet walk. Many towns have rivers running through, som flanked by decaying warehouses or former industrial buildings whic completely block public access. We feel that there should be a positiv policy to establish riverside walkways, as in Stamford, Lincolnshire, wher the Council have cleared the banks, seeded grass and provided seats so tha people can stroll or sit beside the River Welland.

7.40   In London the opportunities are immense, yet where are the plans t enable the public to walk from Westminster to Greenwich, or from Chelse to Hammersmith? Any riverside land becoming available is usuall gobbled up for hotels and offices. It is essential to safeguard at least thirt feet or more on each side of the river or the canal towpaths for the use c the public. This is, for example, already the policy of both the Teessid Corporation, and of the Cardiff City Council, for all rivers and streams i their area.

Canals

7.41   The natural link between town and country is often the canal. There ar 2,000 miles of inland waterways in Great Britain, and their former use fo industry and transportation is giving way to recreation. We were delighte to see the work done to clear the Caldon Canal, leading out of Stoke-on Trent; and in Reading there are plans originating from students at th University, and supported by the Council, to revitalise the Kennet an parts of the Thames. Regents Canal, in London, is very popular and use by many boating enthusiasts, but there should undoubtedly be specia grants to local authorities to clear canals and put locks into working orde so that full use can be made for leisure of this outstanding natural asset Following the disbanding of the British Waterways Board, we hope tha the new structure of Regional Waterway Authorities will keep up th momentum of improvement recently achieved.

Canoeing on the Caldon Canal.

Regent's Canal, City of Westminster.

Parks

7.42 The network of National Parks, areas of outstanding natural beauty, an
over 360,000 acres owned by the National Trust, provide an escape for th
harassed town-dweller, and a source of pleasure to those who live nearby
Yet some people want more than just to enjoy the views or to go for
ramble, and it is difficult to keep small children amused without speci:
attractions.

7.43 Knowsley Park, Liverpool, has a children's area with a roundabout, apa:
from the many wild animals; Blair Drummond Safari Park, at Stirling
Scotland, offers giraffes, zebras, performing dolphins, and boat rides roun
the island; while at Shanes Castle, Antrim, Northern Ireland, there is
miniature train for journeys across the estate. Those particular parks ar
run by private enterprise, but one of the most delightful country parks w
visited was at Coombe Abbey, just five miles from the centre of Coventry
where the City Council have arranged an excellent children's playgroun:
and paddling pool, and angling and boating are available in the lak
beyond the ornamental gardens.

Lions at Blair Drummond, Scotland.

7.44 Nowadays people require more facilities, and we feel it is essential that parks should have cleverly sited and landscaped car parks, well signposted nature trails, picnic areas, and special places for barbecues. There is also a need for yet more parks, as new and expanding towns and an increasing population put more pressure on existing leisure outlets.

7.45 In the County of Fife, Scotland, the systematic reclamation of derelict colliery land will provide, by 1976, a new Country Park of 500 acres in Lochore Meadows at the foot of the Lomond Hills. There will be sailing and boating on a lake, and a golf course nearby. At Winchwen, Swansea, the wholesale planting of trees on former industrial land will make a smaller park. We think that derelict land all over the country unsuitable for building should be reclaimed urgently to make new parks for public enjoyment.

Caravans

7.46 About three million people were caravanners or campers in 1970, but many caravan sites lack showers, hot water, drying rooms and other facilities which are taken for granted on the continent. We found some sites where caravans were crowded closely together and where there were far too few lavatories. We had intended to visit one particular place and were told 'Don't go. It is only a field with a locked gate'. Families who take yearly caravan holidays have told us that many places fall far short of the standards set by the non-profitmaking Caravan Club, and 69% of caravanners interviewed by the British Tourist Authority said they would be prepared to pay extra for improved facilities.

7.47 Another problem is landscaping. Some of our contributors complained that little or no trouble is taken to screen the impact of caravans on the locality, and others were afraid that areas of natural beauty which automatically attract caravanners were in danger of losing their beauty by the visual intrusion of large caravan parks. There are more than 200,000 static holiday caravan sites scattered all over the country, some of which are used as second homes. It is essential that these should be more carefully located. The Friends of the Lake District support a restriction on caravan colours to perhaps green or brown. On the other hand, caravan-users are afraid of road accidents if only dark colours are allowed.

7.48 The most attractive caravan site we visited was Yellowcraig, in East Lothian. Laid out by the Caravan Club, it won a Civic Trust award for the design which incorporated high brushwood hedges to shield the caravans which are parked in groups of twenty. Brooklane, in Ferring-by-Sea, is well landscaped and there are separate areas for older people needing peace and quiet, and for families with young children. Co-operative Woods at Woolwich has a manager who speaks five languages, and among many other excellent facilities, the owners provide electric razor points and

irons. One New Zealand family has returned there every year when visiting Great Britain.

7.49 We feel there should be much stricter control over planning permission granted for new caravan sites; that old planning permissions should be reviewed and in some cases bought out; that the local authorities should use their powers under the Caravan Sites Act 1960 to require proper facilities to be installed; and that landscaping of a high standard should be made obligatory for owners of sites in order to protect the privacy of local residents, and to preserve the environment.

Camping

7.50 Membership of the Camping Club now numbers 113,000 and is increasing all the time. At Chertsey, the non-profit making Camping Club of Great Britain and Ireland, have spent £50,000 on improving the facilities of their twelve acre site and an extra £6,000 in landscaping. It is on the bank of the Thames and will also cater for caravanners. Temporary camping sites are urgently needed for the peak holiday times of July and August. The Race Course Association opened fourteen of their courses in 1971 on non-racing days to both campers and caravanners, following the success of the pilot scheme at Ayr. We think that more summer camping sites could be established in the grounds of Stately Homes, like those already provided at Castle Howard, Yorkshire; Blair Atholl, Perthshire; and Thelowarren, Cornwall.

7.51 It is essential that higher standards should be required for permanent camping sites. We strongly support the suggestion of the Camping Working Party that there should be new planning controls to cover touring caravans and tents. At present there is no limit to the number of tents which can be crammed on to a site for up to twenty eight days in any year. Checking is almost impossible for local authorities and there is often serious infringement of existing laws with resulting risks to the health and safety of visitors.

Open-Air Museums

7.52 Another interesting trend for recreation in the country is the establishment of open-air museums. At Singleton, Sussex, we were fascinated by the many early farm buildings which have been erected on this undulating thirty five acre site. An eighteenth century granary, a timber framed farm house, and a charcoal-burner's hut in the woods have attracted thousands of visitors since the museum opened in 1971. At the Welsh Folk Museum, St Fagans, Wales, there are several farm houses with period furnishings, a tannery, a cockpit, and a gaily-painted gipsy caravan. At Beamish, Co

Sutton Hill, Woodlands Camping Site, Dorset. Camping Club of Great Britain and Ireland. Civic Trust Award 1968.
Camping Site, Fermanagh, Castle Archdale, Northern Ireland.

Durham, there are plans to show coal-mining machinery, railway coaches, and a bow-fronted chemist's shop with the original contents, once owned by John Walker who invented the friction match in 1827. The East Anglian Museum of Rural Life at Stowmarket is in the process of saving early timber-framed buildings from the surrounding area which will be re-erected in their grounds, and this whole concept, besides providing an instant history lesson, is imaginative and appeals to all age-groups.

Tourism

7.53   Tourists account for a good deal of pressure upon outlets for recreation and leisure. Many of our more obvious tourist attractions are over-used, resulting in queues to see the crown jewels, and traffic problems when coach-loads arrive to watch the changing of the guard at Buckingham Palace. Many attractions are under-used such as historic towns or beautiful country villages which could use increased tourist revenue for conservation and improvements. At present, tourists lack information. In towns, enquiry desks are often buried in the depths of the Town Hall, which is both intimidating and time consuming for visitors, whereas kiosks in the middle of the town, as in Cirencester, attract thousands of inquiries and result in satisfied customers. A new point-of-entry bureau has recently been set up at Dover, and there are plans for further bureaux at Folkestone, at Heathrow and Gatwick airports, and the Scottish border.

7.54   We also think that local authorities should be given clear powers in the new Local Government Bill, to operate more comprehensive tourist information centres. These would publicise regional or national attractions, and give details of accommodation of all kinds, to cater especially for the roving tourist.

7.55   The British Tourist Authority, The English, Scottish, Welsh and the Regional Tourist Boards, backed by substantial Government grants, are doing their utmost, not only to help hoteliers, but to establish new tourist outlets. This will also mean improvement of the habitat, provided visitors from home and abroad are kept within reasonable proportions in relation to established residents.

Conclusion

7.56   To cope with the leisure explosion we suggest the following. Greater provision for do-it-yourself holidays now gaining in popularity, since more camping and caravanning, more use of motels and rented chalets, seems to be the trend for the future. More provision for leisure in towns, such as sports centres, and improvements to existing parks to provide tennis

Cockpit at St Fagan's Museum, Cardiff, Wales.

Miniature Railway, Shane's Castle, Northern Ireland.

boating and other games facilities. More quiet places in central areas for old people, tired shoppers, workers in their lunch breaks, or just the passers-by. The canals linking town and country should be cleared to open up a new avenue for recreation. In the country parks, nature trails should be established, and on private land, rights of way should be clearly marked, and ramblers should not upset farmers by straying over crops or private pastures. Local authorities should use more imagination in their whole approach to recreation and leisure and yet not clamp down with the dead hand of officialdom. We may have different ways of using our precious spare time, but we all want to feel, not tired and frustrated, but refreshed and happy, when the moment comes to return to work.

opposite: Fishing on the Grand Union Canal at Marsworth, Hertfordshire.

Gipsy Caravan at St Fagan's Museum, Cardiff, Wales.

Recommendations

39   *Existing parks should have increased facilities for active recreation and be made generally more attractive. Landscaped areas, small gardens and walkways should be created in all our towns.*

40   *In built up areas, the Government should investigate the provision of Leisure and Sports Centres by a partnership of local authorities and private enterprise.*

41   *Museums should have flexible opening times, better lighting, more seats and general comforts. Treasures should be arranged in a more exciting and more artistic way so that visitors would be attracted by the atmosphere of beauty, relaxation and fun.*

42   *Local authorities should clear canals, put locks into working order, and make the best of them for sport and recreation. There should be public access to all river banks and canal towpaths.*

43   *Country parks of all types should be encouraged. Facilities should include landscaped car parks, nature trails and special areas for picnics and barbecues.*

44   *Derelict land unsuitable for building should be more quickly reclaimed for public enjoyment and recreation. Central and local government should combine to step up this work which could vastly improve the urban environment.*

45   *There should be new planning controls to cover touring caravans and tents.*

46   *All caravan and camping sites should be more carefully located, have improved facilities, and better landscaping, in order to protect the interests of both caravanners and local residents.*

8 Environmental Education

Contents

Public Opinion   169

Working Party Opinion   173

The Philosophy   173

Education of Environmental Professionals   175

Education of the Public   176

Conclusion   180

Recommendations   181

8   Public Opinion

8.1   **Terence Gregory** City Architect and Planning Officer, Coventry, Warwickshire

'There is a continuing and deepening need to emphasise the importance of education in relation to conservation and the environment. People must be encouraged to have a real understanding of the causes and the implications of environmental change, and an understanding of the likely effects of an inadequate or negative policy towards conservation. Education will assist in enabling people to understand the consequences of the actions of individuals and of society as a whole, and should generate a keen respect for the environment. The very necessary educative process should not be directed only at the public, young and old, but more especially to those who have responsibilities for decision-making in Local Government. So few people recognise their responsibilities towards a creative approach to the environment.'

8.2   **Lichfield Civic Society** Staffordshire

'The worst feature of a bad environment is that it makes those who live in it insensitive to its worst features. If they did not become immune to dreariness, congestion and confusion they would find life intolerable.'

8.3   **Simon Jenkins** from **'A City at Risk'**

'A city that will rise up in munificent anguish at the prospect of losing such great works of art as a Leonardo cartoon or a Duccio, can still show an appalling apathy towards the disappearance of the uniquely English art that is enshrined in so many London buildings. And while we pummel our school children with endless instruction in the history of painting and sculpture, arts which many of them find alien and to which most of them will never return— we tell them virtually nothing of the art of architecture which they are seeing all about them every hour of the day. It is in failures such as this that the real danger to the future identity of London lies.'

8.4   **Horncastle Civic Society** Lincolnshire

'With all the advances in communication growth, we are still parochial and insular. Local problems are still personal ones, and very few seem to see their town or country as a whole unit. They tend to know their own street or avenue and have a close concern about its well-being, but only look beyond when some other aspect of their daily round is about to be upset like the introduction of a one-way street system.'

8.5 **Countryside Commission for Scotland**

'*The younger generation may not react with the same antipathy as their elders to extensive areas of spruce forest nor to valleys flooded by reservoirs, not having known a countryside of bare hillside, or being perhaps more concerned to find recreational use for inland waters. On the other hand, there is little doubt that an ecological awareness and desire for decisions based on long-term cycling and re-use of natural resources is becoming increasingly widespread as a result of modern resource-based education.*'

8.6 **Taylor Woodrow Property Company** London

'*Education is a key factor in the maintenance of an environment. There must be respect for the privacy of neighbours, their property and their behavioural peculiarities.*'

8.7 **The Countryside in 1970** Extract **Report of the Council for Environmental Education**

'*Environmental education should form an essential part of the education of every citizen. It can permeate a range of disciplines both traditional and new as well as form the mainspring of many integrated courses. To this end, increased collaboration between disciplines is required, whether by interrelating or by integrating their teaching.*

There is an urgent need for more emphasis on environmental education in the training of teachers, initial and in-service, to provide a broader appreciation of environmental issues, as well as specialist knowledge and first-hand experience of field work and countryside lore. Opportunities should be developed for student teachers to assist in outdoor study courses.'

8.8 **Colchester Civic Society** Essex. Cyril Meadows

'*Where academic tuition is not conditioned by concern for good moral behaviour our young people are brainwashed into believing that any cultural or material wealth around them is theirs for the asking and does not have to be earned. Thus is destroyed in them the desire to respect the property of others, the ability to know how best to meet the permanent challenge of nature versus civilisation, and the initiative to help build a better world instead of protesting that others must do it for them.*'

8.9 **Weald of Kent Preservation Society**

'*Not nearly enough attention is being paid by practising architects and schools of architecture to the quality of design in rural areas. We believe that improvements can only come through education through the profession to the public. We therefore consider that personnel should be trained in rural design, including the design of farm buildings, with a view to improving on the present suburban, townified standards being perpetuated in and around villages. And that such personnel, when trained, should act as consultants to councils for the purpose of deciding all rural development on design grounds before the granting of planning permission.'*

8.10   **Baroness Sharp** Extract from **'Transport Planning'** 1970
'I feel sure that the people engaged in transport planning should be interchangeable with those engaged in land-use planning; and that what is really in issue is the development of a corps of people with a wide variety of education, training and experience to work in the whole spectrum of environmental planning, and to be members of a single society in which all can meet to discuss their common problems. I am well aware of the difficulties in this; difficulties arising from the wide variety of skills which must contribute to the total complex of environmental planning. But I believe that unless it is done planning will not be adequately served.'

overpage: Brighton Square, Sussex.

8   Working Party Opinion

The Philosophy

8.11   The environment in town and country is no longer something to be taken for granted with indifference or at worst a shrug of discontent. We have awoken to the fact that we can consciously spoil or improve it, and that we are all responsible.

8.12   This new environmental consciousness is accompanied by confusion about ways and means, and by uncertainty as to what precisely we want to achieve. Without better understanding of our total environment, we cannot solve the complex problems of managing and conserving it. Yet can the study of the environment fit into the modern pattern of education, and can it become an accepted academic subject, with a syllabus, examinations, and an appropriate teaching structure?

8.13   Rural studies have been taught in some schools since the beginning of the century but nowadays they are clearly inadequate as a basis for the study of the total environment in an overwhelmingly urban society. But it is doubtful if the real purposes of environmental education can be fulfilled by the development of a new subject along the lines of Rural Studies but called 'Environmental Studies'—complete with its own concepts, techniques and values, and taught like history or geography or languages at every level of education from the primary school to the research institute. For one thing, such a subject might well kill off the vital ability to enjoy the environment. Both understanding and appreciation of the environment may rather be achieved by drawing out the environmental implications of many different areas of study—as a road engineer comes to see his work as only one element in the whole pattern of urban life, or an architect conceives his new designs in relation to the existing structure of a town.

8.14   But environmental education cannot just be a matter of teaching people to see the environmental aspects of their particular subject. They must also learn judgement and discrimination. Education is pre-eminently a matter of realising values. Environmental education should be part of the moral and aesthetic education of the human being as a whole.

8.15   It may affect his behaviour in at least two ways. First, it can correct ignorance about facts. A person who has been taught which species of wild flowers are most rare and most endangered by indiscriminate picking, has been given a part of the intellectual equipment required to control his influence over the environment. At the same time, it should help him to form a moral judgement about whether or not to pick flowers which his

Coombe Abbey, Community Park, Coventry.

knowledge tells him are rare. He is also left with a choice, for education must not be used as a form of propaganda. Environmental education is not only a matter of learning how to conserve the physical environment, since there are alternative views about the importance of conservation. It is essential to realise that the human habitat is not just a world of objects: it is a world of values. The moral purpose of environmental education is to enable the citizen to understand those values, to criticise them, and where necessary to change them.

Education of Environmental Professionals

8.16   Environmental education may have its greatest immediate effect through the education of the professional and technical men and women who are engaged in day-to-day work which can affect the environment. Good citizenship among the decision-makers is even more important than among the general public. It is now being accepted that there is a special group of land-linked professions concerned with the planning, management and development of the natural resources of land, air and water. This relationship has been recognised by the introduction of common first and second year courses in some of the institutions which provide professional training. An interdisciplinary approach has been adopted in the teaching of these courses, reflecting the type of team-work that is increasingly being adopted in the management of the environment.

8.17   There is also a growing emphasis on practical and project work. Projects are particularly important when they demonstrate the existence of conflict of interest, and the nature of compromise and balance. In this field a valuable exercise was the 'Study in Countryside Conservation' undertaken in 1968 by officers of the Hampshire County Council and Government agencies, in the East Hampshire Area of Outstanding Natural Beauty.

8.18   The 'Countryside in 1970' report on Professional and Technical Services, describes the progress made in establishing the principles of environmental management in professional and academic qualifying courses since 1965. Nevertheless, there is a rising sense of frustration at certain provisions in the codes of practice of the existing professions, which tend to hinder the formation of inter-professional partnerships. There is also a growing interest in the development of a new professional group of specialist 'environmental managers', but until environmental management has been further developed as a definite occupation with distinctive educational requirements, it will be difficult to find room for graduates with a specialised training in environmental studies.

8.19   It may be possible to resolve some of these difficulties by providing special centres for teaching and research in disciplines connected with the environment. 'The Countryside in 1970' report on the professions shows that in the field of environmental studies the same proliferation of courses is developing as was identified by Lady Sharp in the training of transport

175

planners. She recommended that these courses should be concentrated in a number of centres. This might reduce the impact of the environmental consciousness across the whole range of studies not intimately connected with environmental management. But it would offer corresponding advantages in the organisation of interdisciplinary work, and in the strength and depth of the studies that would emerge. It would also make it easier to provide better opportunities for mid-career education. In central institutions the necessary cross-links could more easily be built up with local and central government as well as with private bodies.

8.20   In 'Transport Planning', Lady Sharp writes: 'The course ought to include something I can only describe as "urban values"; since the transport planner must be a man who realises that the optimum plan for transport may not be, and probably is not, the right plan—that what finally matters is the total environment in which peace and quiet and civilised surround ings may be valued more highly than the ability to get around fast'. This emphasis on values is important: environmental education for the pro fessionals is also a branch of moral and aesthetic education, just as much as it is a training in specialised techniques.

8.21   The professional man is not merely the passive instrument of economic and political processes which dictate the character of his work. Nor is the only source of a technician's failure to be found in some deficiency of technique. Planners have a bad name, not because of their inability to control the forces of progress but because they are often rightly felt to be the willing agents and indeed initiators of unwelcome and inhuman developments. Technique tempered by humility should be the watchword for the new integrated corps of planners.

Education of the Public

8.22   In the schools, environmental studies are still underdeveloped. There is also a shortage of teacher training facilities. Although there are now five colleges of education which offer B.Ed degrees with a general environment label, they are still greatly outnumbered by the seventeen colleges pro viding B.Eds in rural studies. It is difficult both to give status to environ mental studies and to find room for them on the timetable. They are still considered in many schools to be a subject suitable for non-examination classes only. They do not at the moment attract either the best teachers or the more academic pupils who may be the decision-takers of the future.

8.23   The establishment of adequate standards of environmental education in the schools is linked with the development of standards in higher and further education. In principle the issues are the same, although their treatment at the higher levels is necessarily more advanced and complicated. Can environmental studies be a subject in their own right or must they emerge from a set of integrated, interdisciplinary courses?

The Giles, Pittenweem, Fife, before restoration.

The Giles, Pittenweem, Fife, after restoration.

The High Street, Southend-on-Sea, after pedestrianisation.

8.24   In higher education the creation of a number of national centres offers a possible way out of this dilemma. This solution is not available in schools. There is consequently growing pressure to invest environmental education with all the required panoply of academic syllabuses and examinations. The new Certificate of Secondary Education already offers some examination courses in the environment; and Mode 3 examinations—set and marked by individual schools according to syllabuses of their own devising —are being used. Developments in the General Certificate of Education have been slower, but there are now four Boards offering Ordinary Level papers in rural or environmental studies. But the problems are more acute at Advanced Level—where the examinations provide the basis for University entrance. Teachers in Hertfordshire have been striving to devise an 'A' level syllabus in environmental studies, and at the end of 1970 a conference was held at Offley bringing together representatives of the Universities, the Examination Boards, the teachers and the professional bodies.

8.25   Meanwhile, there are changes in the traditional subjects which provide an important element in environmental studies in the schools. Biology and geography are shifting their boundaries, and more fieldwork and practical enquiry are being undertaken. But it will be difficult to establish environmental studies as a coherent subject. Despite its optimism this was very apparent at the Offley Conference: 'Before us is a very wide spectrum. Perhaps at the one end we have matters of sociological concern; at the other end, interest in the natural environment from the point of view of strict ecological studies. Between these extremes lie studies of the rural and urban environment. In depth we vary from the world-wide picture to the local scene.'

8.26   Apart from the concept of the academic syllabus there is developing another and perhaps more fruitful approach: the development of environmental education as an education in awareness. Art education provides one important avenue. Since they are both the subject of visual appreication there is a natural link between art and the environment.

8.27   There are also other forms of practical activity which are designed to develop a more intense social awareness. Fieldwork is a concept made familiar by rural studies. Its urban counterpart is street-work. Practical environmental projects in the countryside, such as the study of the effect of the M4 motorway in Wiltshire, must be extended into learning about the urban environment and its development.

8.28   Perhaps urban centres for environmental studies at school level might be established, along the lines already so successful in the countryside. Many school-leavers are ill-equipped to understand how their society works. A deeper understanding of the complexity and diversity of these processes might produce not merely a generation of citizens with a greater critical awareness, but also a generation of planners with a better understandin of the complex of interrelated social and physical elements which make u the living environment.

Conclusion

8.29 We feel that environmental education is essentially a form of civic edu cation. It is education for good citizenship. It is closely related to th development of a more advanced environmental consciousness in th general public. It is also related to the character of the political processe by which the environment is governed. As our essay on People and Plan ing points out, officials and local politicians who take environment; decisions should have a more advanced understanding of what they ar doing. The public must be given the opportunity to acquire throug practical experience both the awareness and the capacity to play a decisiv part in environmental decision-making.

8.30 Over the last few years there has undoubtedly been an enormous growt in the public's awareness of environmental issues. The proliferation c films, radio and television programmes, local and national newspape articles, as well as the work carried out in European Conservation Yea have all had a significant influence.

8.31 But there is a need for more research into the ways in which publi opinion on environmental issues has developed. We suggest that th Department of the Environment should study the reasons for the succes of the anti-litter campaign, or for the rapid growth of the movement fc the conservation of historic buildings. As a form of education withou tears, environmental issues could be dramatised in a fictional televisio serial. We also suggest that the Department of the Environment shoul make a continuing series of films on every aspect of our habitat, whic could be sent to all schools and institutes of higher education. They coul be shown on closed circuit television, just as films on 'Tomorrow's Glasgov were shown in eighteen Glasgow schools. We think that a Nationa Information Centre and a Central Intelligence Unit along the lines sug gested by the 'Countryside in 1970' report, would help to improve contac between those especially concerned with the environment, and would als improve the quality of information which is diffused among a wider publi

8.32 Ultimately the best form of environmental education for the citizen is th exercise of citizenship itself. The development of opportunities for re sponsible participation in the process by which environmental decision are made, is a far more important form of education than anything that ca be provided either by the media of communications, or by the institutior of formal academic instruction. The beginning and the end of a successf environmental education is a lively and articulate democracy.

Recommendations

47 *Environmental education and the exercise of citizenship go hand in hand: the opening-up of opportunities for public participation in decision-making is the most important of all means to environmental education, which should aim at developing a critical, moral and aesthetic awareness of our surroundings.*

48 *The professional organisations and the institutions of environmental education at the professional level should review their practices and encourage a more effective interdisciplinary team-work approach. Their policies towards professional education should be in line with the interdisciplinary requirements of environmental management. Opportunities should be extended for the mid-career education of professionals in environmental studies.*

49 *School children must be encouraged to learn about the environment in practical ways. Project work, both in the rural and in the urban environment, should become more wide-spread at all levels of ability. Consideration should be given to the establishment of urban centres for environmental study, along the lines already familiar in countryside studies.*

50 *There should be a wider application of team-teaching methods to the study of the environment, bringing together the perspectives of different subjects and different teachers, in which the art department has a special role to play.*

51 *Audiovisual methods should be more widely used. Perhaps the resources and expertise of the Department of the Environment and the Open University might be applied to the production of a much greater variety of high quality films, tapes and other materials for environmental education in further education and in the schools.*

52 *There should be more research into the means by which the general public forms its attitudes to environmental issues, and the lesson incorporated into teacher-training courses.*

53   *Television companies should think hard about the possibility*
     dramatising environmental issues in popular television fictio
54   *Decision-makers in both local and national government shou*
     be given more opportunity to learn about how their decisio
     can affect the environment, and a National Centre should
     created to service this and all other aspects of environment
     education.

Restored shop front, High Street, Haddington.

pothecary's Shop, North of England Open Air Museum, Beamish, Co. Durham.

Epilogue

Welcome as it is to find public opinion awakening to the value of outdoor environment in town and country, we have to face the fact that frustration and disillusionment await us unless sweeping changes can be achieved in the attitude and sense of values of both individuals and society. For example, well-intentioned efforts to determine by the crudest kind of cost-benefit how to decide planning issues may well be bracketed by our descendants with the arguments of medieval theologians over the number of angels who could dance on the point of a needle.

Much of our leisure and tourist traffic is essentially a refugee flight from the intolerable habitats which we have permitted to grow up in our cities, and which, in the course of that flight, become duplicated in our holiday retreats. Piecemeal and artificial spasms of conservation and preservation, neglecting the essential need to bring about a genuine harmony between people and people as well as between people and their habitat, will yield little satisfaction or sense of fulfilment. Our faces reflect what we have made of ourselves in our lives: our landscapes and townscapes reflect the quality of our society. All must be made to understand that if these are squalid and degraded, we cannot escape the same judgement on ourselves. They must be accorded a full share of whatever pride and self-respect we can muster for whatever we most firmly believe in. If we can learn to identify ourselves with our environment, we will be nearer to answering rightly the question, 'How do we want to live?'

MAX NICHOLSON

p. 186: Regent's Canal, City of Westminster.

opposite: The Rows, Chester.

Summary of Recommendations

People and Planning

1 *When planning authorities consult interested parties on planning decisions, they should offer alternatives. The financial and environmental consequences must be made clear and the choice should be put before the public in simple language.*

2 *There should be a specific, universal, and named procedure to give local publicity to all planning proposals beyond the merely trivial.*

3 *It should be standard practice for outside representatives to be co-opted on to local planning committees.*

4 *The Press should also be admitted to planning committees; all non-elected persons could be asked to leave when delicate financial matters are being discussed.*

5 *The Department of the Environment, together with the Civic Trust, the Town and Country Planning Association, and other bodies, should make a series of films on different aspects of planning to be shown to local authorities throughout the country.*

6 *The Government should amend the laws relating to compensation:*
   a *so that property just outside the line of a new road, but seriously affected by it, can be acquired.*
   b *To enable grants to be made to owners for sound-proofing and similar work without acquisition.*
   c *To allow more flexibility in assessing compensation payable to small traders who at present suffer hardship due to redevelopment of their area, or due to other planning decisions.*

Housing and Architecture

7 *The Government should offer additional financial incentives to encourage rehabilitation and environmental improvements in older housing areas; and to encourage the return of a resident population to the centres of our towns and cities.*

8   *The Government should give extra financial encouragement for the improvement of individual dwellings, and rate increases on improved houses should be delayed for five years.*

9   *The development of virgin land should be more strictly controlled, especially where there is derelict or under-utilised land in urban areas.*

10   *The Government should give new incentives to ensure that social facilities and landscaping are provided to coincide with the completion of new housing projects.*

11   *The architectural profession should instigate further research into the design of homes which could be easily expanded or contracted according to the changing needs of the occupants.*

12   *Architectural competitions should be encouraged.*

13   *We suggest that the Secretary of State for the Environment sends a circular to all local planning authorities urging them to interpret the existing Planning Acts for the maximum protection and enhancement of the habitat.*

Conservation Areas and Historic Buildings

14   *We welcome the new proposals for legislation for the greater protection of unlisted buildings in conservation areas.*

15   *Local authorities should follow the example of the Government by establishing a cleaning fund for the regular cleaning of public buildings; they should give owners percentage grants from this fund towards the cost of cleaning privately-owned buildings.*

16   *Each local authority should set up a special sub-committee of their planning committee with its own budget, to be concerned with conservation, historic buildings, and town improvements.*

17   *Suitable measures should be taken to increase the supply of architects, builders and craftsmen with skills in the repair and adaptation of historic buildings.*

18   *The new District Councils should take urgent steps to obtain skilled professional advice on the historic buildings which will become their responsibility. In some cases they could use County Council staff as their agents. Under the act, the Secretary of State for the Environment should require District*

Councils to make arrangements which he considers to be satisfactory.

19 *We also ask the Government to reconsider that part of the new legislation which removes all historic buildings powers from County Councils. There should, however, be opportunities for preservation at both levels of local government, provided that the arrangements of the authorities concerned satisfy the Secretary of State.*

20 *More Historic Building Trusts, and a National Buildings Conservation Fund, should be established without delay.*

21 *The Government should consider the whole question of tax rebates and estate duty in relation to historic buildings.*

Traffic

22 *Local authorities should not allow town centres to be used as through roads for traffic. 'Loop' and other systems should be examined for confining through traffic to circumferential roads.*

23 *More ring roads should be developed, to allow as many streets as possible within the ring to be physically closed to through traffic.*

24 *Local authorities should examine schemes of neighbourhood environmental management for the exclusion of local through traffic from residential areas in towns and cities.*

25 *Local authorities should exercise powers to control and restrict town centre parking, since this is the most effective way of limiting car commuting.*

26 *The Government should accept the principle of public subsidy of public transport. Only if public transport undertakings receive suitable funds for development can they continue to play their part in holding down the social costs of urban congestion.*

27 *Private bus operators should be more freely licensed to provide services in deprived rural and suburban areas.*

28 *More local authorities should introduce reserved bus lanes to speed the flow of public transport.*

29 *Foot streets should be established without delay in all towns and cities.*

Industry and Commerce

30   *Because of the growing scale of industrial plant and the tendency to agglomerate, the cumulative effect should be anticipated by assessing the environmental capacity of an area to absorb them.*

31   *With so many major industrial installations gravitating to the coast and towards deep water facilities, a policy of development inland from these points should be adopted whenever possible, rather than to allow industrial growth to proliferate along the coastline.*

32   *In areas of commercial pressure the capacity of the area to contain massive increases in office floor space should be more strictly assessed, with a greater emphasis on the environmental consequences.*

33   *While recognising the need for changes in the structure of retailing, major out-of-town shopping centres or hyper-markets should only be allowed in exceptional cases and where no damage to existing nearby town centres would result.*

34   *There should be a faster rehabilitation of inherited areas of dereliction, more assistance to local authorities whose areas have suffered economic decline as a result, and grants for rehabilitation of derelict land in private or in industrial ownership.*

35   *The National Farmers Union and the Department of the Environment should co-operate to draw up a form of planning control for farm buildings.*

36   *We recommend greater research be undertaken into energy transmission methods and transportation of products, with particular reference to the transmission of electrical power and underground pipelines.*

37   *In economic policies towards depressed areas, greater efforts should be made to achieve positive environmental improvements.*

38   *There should be a general shift of emphasis from predominantly economic and technical, to social and human criteria, for new development of all kinds.*

Recreation

39 *Existing parks should have increased facilities for active recreation and be made generally more attractive. Landscaped areas, small gardens and walkways should be created in all our towns.*

40 *In built up areas, the Government should investigate the provision of Leisure and Sports Centres by a partnership of local authorities and private enterprise.*

41 *Museums should have flexible opening times, better lighting, more seats and general comforts. Treasures should be arranged in a more exciting and more artistic way so that visitors would be attracted by the atmosphere of beauty, relaxation and fun.*

42 *Local authorities should clear canals, put locks into working order, and make the best of them for sport and recreation. There should be public access to all river banks and canal towpaths.*

43 *Country parks of all types should be encouraged. Facilities should include landscaped car parks, nature trails and special areas for picnics and barbecues.*

44 *Derelict land unsuitable for building should be more quickly reclaimed for public enjoyment and recreation. Central and local government should combine to step up this work which could vastly improve the urban environment.*

45 *There should be new planning control to cover touring caravans and tents.*

46 *All caravan and camping sites should be more carefully located, have improved facilities, and better landscaping, in order to protect the interests of both caravanners and local residents.*

Environmental Education

47 *Environmental education and the exercise of citizenship go hand in hand: the opening-up of opportunities for public participation in decision-making is the most important of all means to environmental education, which should aim at developing a critical, moral and aesthetic awareness of our surroundings.*

48   *The professional organisations and the institutions of environ mental education at the professional level should review thei practices and encourage a more effective interdisciplinary team-work approach. Their policies towards professiona education should be in line with the interdisciplinary require ments of environmental management. Opportunities should b extended for the mid-career education of professionals ir environmental studies.*

49   *School children must be encouraged to learn about the environ ment in practical ways. Project work, both in the rural and ir the urban environment, should become more widespread at al levels of ability. Consideration should be given to the establish ment of urban centres for environmental study, along the line. already familiar in countryside studies.*

50   *There should be a wider application of team-teaching method. to the study of the environment, bringing together the per spectives of different subjects and different teachers, in whic the art department has a special role to play.*

51   *Audiovisual methods should be more widely used. Perhaps the resources and expertise of the Department of the Environmen and the Open University might be applied to the production of a much greater variety of high quality films, tapes and other materials for environmental education in further education and in the schools.*

52   *There should be more research into the means by which the general public forms its attitudes to environmental issues, and the lesson incorporated into teacher-training courses.*

53   *Television companies should think hard about the possibility of dramatising environmental issues in popular television fiction.*

54   *Decision-makers in both local and national government should be given more opportunity to learn about how their decisions can affect the environment, and a National Centre should be created to service this and all other aspects of environmental education.*

Contributors who wrote direct or gave us permission to use extracts from their writings or papers

Alexander, Christopher
Amos, Francis
Ampthill and District Preservation Society
Andrews, Raymond
Arts Council of Great Britain
Arup, Sir Ove
Association of Municipal Corporations
Association of River Authorities
Automobile Association
Aylsham Association
Baily, Michael
Banham, Professor Reyner
Barker, Paul
Barking, London Borough of
Barnet, London Borough of
Batsford, Brian MP
Bennet, Pamela K
Bexley, London Borough of
Bland, E A
Blythe, K G
Board for Social Responsibility
Bradford Civic Society
Brentwood Civic Society
Brewood Civic Society
Briggs, Professor Asa
British Film Institute
British Mountaineering Council
British Railways Board
British Steel Corporation
British Tourist Authority
Brockham Green Village Society
Brooke Society
Browne, Kenneth
Bruton Trust
Buchanan, Professor Sir Colin
Burleigh Housing Association
Burley Village Protection Society
Burke, Gerald
Burnley and District Civic Trust
Burtons St Leonards Society
Calder Civic Trust
Caldon Canal Society
Camblin, Gilbert
Cambridge Planning Interface Trust
Campden Trust
Camping Club of Great Britain and Ireland
Canterbury Society

Caravan Club of Great Britain and Ireland
Carlton Club
Carmunnock Preservation Society
Carson, S Mc B—Environment Education
    Officer, Herts
Cave, Lyndon
Central Electricity Generating Board
Central Gardens Association
Centre for Economic and Social
    Information
Centre for Environmental Studies
Charlton Society
Chedworth Society
Chelmsford Society
Chelsea Society
Cirencester Civic Society
City of London
Civic Society of Otley
Civic Society of St Ives
Civic Trust for the North East
Civic Trust for the North West
Civic Trust for Wales
Clandon Society
Clark, Lord
Claverdon Village Preservation Society
Cleary, F E
Cockburn, Miss
Colchester Civic Society
Coleshill Civic Society
Committee for the Protection of Rural Kent
Confederation of British Industry
Conservation Society
Corbusier, Le
Council of Engineering Institutions
Council of Industrial Design
Council for Nature
Council for the Protection of Rural
    England, Head Office
CPRE Berkshire
CPRE Devon
CPRE Dorset
CPRE Hampshire
CPRE Hampshire—Winchester Area
CPRE Lancashire
CPRE Leeds and Lower Dales
CPRE North Staffs
CPRE Oxfordshire

CPRE Scarborough and Pickering
CPRE Somerset
CPRE Warwickshire
Council for the Protection of Rural Wales
Country Landowners Association
Countryside Commission
Countryside Commission for Scotland
County Councils Association
Coventry, City of
Cowan, Peter
Cowburn, William
Crofters Commission Scotland
Crosby, Theo
Crosland, Antony MP
Crown Estates Commissioners
Cunliffe, Mitzi
Cyclists Touring Club
Daniell, Philip
Dartmoor Preservation Association
Deal Society
Denington, Mrs Evelyn
Denman, Professor D R, University of
   Cambridge
Dinas Powis Civic Trust
Don Valley Rural Amenities Association
Dorking and Leith Hill District
   Preservation Society
Dulwich Society
Durham County Council
Dutton, Ralph
East Lothian County Council
Edinburgh, HRH The Duke of
Edwards, A M
English Tourist Board
Eynsford Village Society
Fairfield Halls, Croydon
Farm and Food Society
Faversham Borough Council
Fawkes, Mrs Diana
Fife County Council
Freeman, Dr Hugh
French, Mrs Mary
Friends of the Lake District
Friends of St Ives
Friends of the Vale of Aylesbury
Gardiner, Stephen
Georgian Group
Georgian Society for East Yorkshire
Gnosall Civic Society
Godalming Trust
Golding, Henry
Gower Society
Grant, Ian
Greater London Council

Greenwich, London Borough of
Gregory, Terence
Groves, M M
Guttenburg, Albert Z
Haddington, Royal Borough of
Hall, Peter
Hammersmith, London Borough of
Hammerson Group of Companies
Hampshire County Council, Planning
   Department
Hampshire County Council, Physical
   Fabric and Social Facilities Group
Hampstead Garden Suburb Residents
Hargraves, June
Harris, Peter J
Harrow Hill Trust
Harrow, London Borough of
Haslemere and District Preservation Society
Haslemere Estates Limited
Heath and Old Hampstead Society
Hettena, Trish
Highfield, M H
High Wycombe Society
Hillingdon, London Borough of
Horncastle Civic Society
Horsham Society
Horsley Countryside Preservation Society
Hounslow, London Borough of
House Builders Federation
Humphries, John
Hurley Preservation Society
Hurstpierpoint Preservation Society
Ilkley Civic Society
Imperial Chemical Industries, Brown J C
Inland Waterways Association
Institute of Directors
Institute of Housing Managers
Institution of Civil Engineers
Ipswich Society
Islington, London Borough of
Islington Society
Jacobs, Jane
Jenkins, Graham C
Johnson, A
Joint Committee, The
Jones, Professor D
Jones, Emrys
Judson, Tom
Keep Britain Tidy
Kennet and Avon Canal Trust
Kensington and Chelsea, Royal Borough of
Kenwright, Harold
Kingston Upon Thames, Royal Borough of
Knutsford Society

Leatherhead and District Countryside Protection Society
Leeds—City Development Officer
Leighton Buzzard and District Preservation Society
Levy, Elliot
Lewisham, London Borough of
Lichfield Civic Society
Lincoln Civic Trust
Lincolnshire Association
Lithgow, Sir William
Liverpool University—School of Architecture
Liverpool, City of
Llantrisant Civic Society
Llewelyn-Davies, Lord
Ludlow Society
Lymington Society
MacManus, F & Sons
Madron, Roy
Manningtree and District Amenity Society
Margate Civic Society
Marter, Dr G
Mason, Peter
McConaghy, Des
McLeish, Gordon
Meadows, Cyril
Meopham Society
Mersea Island Society
Merton Civic Society
Merton, London Borough of
Metropolitan Water Board
Midhurst Society
Minster Civic Society
Ministry of Development, Northern Ireland
Moore B P
Moriet, Peter
Morris, Desmond
Museums Association
Museum of Lincolnshire Life
National Council of Women of Great Britain
National Farmers Union of Scotland
National Federation of Housing Societies
National Federation of Women's Institutes
National House Builders Registration Council
National Trust, The (Committee for Northern Ireland)
National Union of Journalists
National Union of Railwaymen
National Union of Townswomen's Guilds
Nature Conservancy
Nature Reserve Committee, N'thern Ireland

Newham, London Borough of
New Mills Amenity Society Cheshire
Nicholson, Max
North Bedfordshire Preservation Society
Northenden Civic Society
Northern Ireland Joint Electricity Authority
North West Kent Federation of Townswomen's Guilds
North Wiltshire Society
Norwich City of Planning Department
Norwich Society
Norwood Society
Owen, T A
Oxford Preservation Trust
Oxted & Limpsfield Amenities Association
Page, Professor J K
Pahl, Professor R E
Pedestrians Association for Road Safety
Pershore Civic Society
Petersfield Society
Pevsner, Sir Nicklaus
Plymouth Humanist Group
Plympton and District Civic Society
Pontefract and District Civic Trust
Porter, Professor Sir George
Portsmouth, City of
Price, Cedric
Pyper, Thomas
Ramblers Association
Rayleigh Civic Society
Reading College of Technology
Reading Waterways Steering Committee
Redbridge, London Borough of
Reigate Society
Reilly, Sir Paul
Renway Construction Ltd
Richmond upon Thames, London Borough of
Richmond Society
River Thames Society
Roberts, Hugh
Rochford Hundred Amenities Society
Rotherham Civic Society
Royal Automobile Club
Royal College of Physicians and Surgeons of Glasgow
Royal Horticultural Society
Royal Institute of British Architects
Royal Institute of Public Administration
Royal Institution of Chartered Surveyors
Royal Society of Arts
Royal Society of Health
Royal Society for the Prevention of Accidents

Royal Society for the Protection of Birds
Roydon Society
Ruislip/Northwood Natural History
Society
Saltford Avon Valley Executive Committee
Sanderstead Preservation Society
Sauchiehall Street Traders Association,
Glasgow
Savage, Dr
Scottish Civic Trust
Scottish Council—Development and
Industry
Scottish Landowners' Federation
Sharp, Baroness
Shelter—Neighbourhood Action Project
(Liverpool)
Shepherd, Peter
Smith, Harold
Society for the Promotion of Nature
Reserves
Society of Sussex Downsmen
Southampton Civic Trust
South Bedfordshire Preservation Society
South Cerney Trust
Southgate Civic Trust
Southwark, London Borough of
Sports Council
Stafford Historical and Civic Society
Staffordshire County Council
St Agnes Amenity Society
St Fagans Village Association
Stanmore Society
Stephens, David
Stevenage Development Corporation
Strand-on-the-Green Association
Stratford-upon-Avon Society
Suffolk Preservation Society
Sunderland Civic Society
Sutton, London Borough of
Swansea Civic Society
Swimbridge Conservation Society
Tamar Protection Society
Tamar Valley Preservation Society
Taylor Woodrow Property Company Ltd
Tenterden Trust
Tetbury Civic Society
Tewkesbury Civic Society
Thaxted Society
Theatrical Management Association
Thompson, Mrs T A
Tonbridge Civic Society
Tower Hamlets Society
Town and Country Planning Association
Trades Union Congress

Truro Civic Society
Ulster Architectural Heritage Society
Ulster Countryside Commission
Ulster Farmers Union
University College, Cardiff
University College of Wales, Aberystwyth
University of Wales
University of Wales—Institute of Science
and Technology
University of York/Rationalist Press
Association
Victorian Society
Wandsworth, London Borough of
Wanstead Residents Society
Ware Society
Wates Ltd
Weald of Kent Preservation Society
Weddle, A E
Westerham Society
West London Architectural Society
Westminster, City of, Department of
Architecture and Planning
Westminster Society
Weymouth Civic Society
Whaley Bridge Amenity Society
Whinney, Margaret
Whitaker, Ben
Wiggins, David
Windsor and Eton Society
Wirral Green Belt Council
Wirral Society
Witham and Countryside Society
Wivenhoe Society
Woburn Sands and District Society
Woledge, H S
Women's Group on Public Welfare
Woodley and Earley Society
Worcester Civic Society
Worcestershire Building Preservation Trust
Ltd
Yeomans, George

Acknowledgements for the Photographs

Glantees Farm, Newton-on-the-Moor. Not known.
Imperial Chemical Industries, Wilton Works, Teesside. ICI.

The Thames at Strand-on-the-Green. Picture Point.
Eardisland, Herefordshire. J Allen Cash.
Preston Oatmeal Mill, East Linton, Scotland. The Scotsman.
The Sea Front at Eastbourne, Sussex. Picture Point.

Little Moreton Hall, near Congleton, Cheshire. Barnaby's Picture Library.
New Offices incorporating Church Tower at Park Circus, Glasgow. Glasgow Corporation.
New Housing in Ross's Close, Haddington, East Lothian. John Dewar.
Bourton-on-the-Water, Gloucestershire. BTA.
The Upper Pedestrian Shopping Precinct, Coventry. City of Coventry.
Carshalton Ponds, Sutton, Surrey. GLC.

Infill Housing at the Old Town, Corby, Northamptonshire. Corby Dev. Corp.
Backcauseway, Culross, Fife. Henk Snoek.
Model of Proposed Scheme for St Katherine-by-the-Tower, London. Henk Snoek.
Marygate Development, Royal Burgh of Pittenweem, Fife. Rolland, Architects.
The Brunton Hall, Musselburgh, Scotland. A L Hunter.
The Raith Housing Estate, Kirkcaldy, Fife. Winner of Civic Trust Award. Henk Snoek.
Aerial view of connecting courts in "The Triangle", Cirencester. Michell and Partners.
Old People's Flats at Broomfield Green, Liverpool City Council. Civic Trust Award 1960. City of Liverpool.

Eighteenth Century Rum Warehouses, Deptford. Turned into flats by the Greater London Council. GLC.
Restored Houses in New Street, Plymouth. Plymouth Barbican Association.
Norton Village Green, Co. Durham. Conservation Area. Teesside CC.
Lifford Street, Putney. Conservation Area. Alan Smith.
Mumbles Village Lane, Swansea, Wales. Conservation Area. Swansea Civic Society.
Infilling of shops in Llandaff High Street, Cardiff. Conservation Area. Wyndham Powell.
36 Looe Street, Plymouth—before restoration. Plymouth Barbican Association.
36 Looe Street, Plymouth—after restoration. Plymouth Barbican Association.
Entrance to shopping precinct through Old George Mall, Salisbury. City of Salisbury.
Christ Church Library, Oxford—before restoration. Thomas Photos.
Christ Church Library, Oxford—after restoration. Thomas Photos.
Members of Working Party and Officials at Tenterden, Kent. Kent Messenger.
The Town Hall Manchester, built by Alfred Waterhouse. City of Manchester.
St Martin-at-Palace Plain, Norwich—before restoration. Norwich CC.
St Martin-at-Palace Plain, Norwich—after restoration. Norwich CC.
Church House, Clare, Suffolk. Restored with grant from Historic Buildings Council. National Monuments Board.
Abbey Mills Pumping Station, Newham, London. GLC.
St Peter's in the East, Oxford. Now a library for St Edmund Hall. Thomas Photos.
Sixteenth Century Building used by Lloyds Bank at Henley-in-Arden, Warwickshire. Lloyds Bank.
Lavenham, Suffolk, before removal of overhead wires. Eastern Electricity Board.
Lavenham, Suffolk, after removal of overhead wires. Eastern Electricity Board.
Dirleton Village and Green, East Lothian. Conservation Area. J Dewar.

Sussex Place, Regent's Park, before restoration by The Crown Commissioners. B & N Westwood.
Sussex Place, Regent's Park, after restoration by The Crown Commissioners. B & N Westwood.

Oak Lane Bridge, Sevenoaks By-Pass A21. Civic Trust Award 1968. Catling Photos.
Motorway crossing The Lune Gorge, South from Borrowbeck. Scott. Wilson. Kirkpatrick.
Traffic Congestion, Conway, Wales. Glam. Conway.
Traffic Congestion, York. Civic Trust.
London Street, Norwich, before pedestrianisation. Norwich CC.
London Street, Norwich, after pedestrianisation. Norwich CC.
The Southern End of Hertford Street, Coventry, before pedestrianisation. City of Coventry.
The Southern End of Hertford Street, Coventry, after pedestrianisation. City of Coventry.
Landscaping at Victoria Park Interchange, Glasgow. Glasgow Corporation.

Paddington Maintenance Depot, Greater London Council. Civic Trust Award 1970. GLC.
The Welsh Glass Works, Swansea, Wales. Swansea CBC.
Yardley Factory, Basildon. Peter L. Sexton.
Portsmouth Building Society Offices. Civic Trust Award 1969. Civic Trust.
Cockenzie Power Station, Scotland. Civic Trust Award. Henk Snoek.
St Helen's Office Building, London. Civic Trust Award 1970. GLC.
Fincham Hall Barn, Norfolk. W A J Spear.
Gas Works, Llandarcy, Glamorgan. RIBA Regional Award 1966. A Gordon.
Raschel Knitting Factory, Swansea. Civic Trust Award. Tempest.
Kodak Building, Hemel Hempstead. Bovis.

Whitworth Art Gallery, University of Manchester. Whitworth Art Gallery.
The Maltings Concert Hall, Snape, Suffolk. Civic Trust Award 1968. Civic Trust.
The River Thames at Corporation Park, near Reading Bridge. Reading CBC.
Theatre at the Forum, Billingham. Teesside Corp.
The Theatre Royal, York. P Gwenne.
The Dry Ski Slope, Crystal Palace, London. GLC.
Toy Display, Bethnal Green Museum. V&A
Roberts' Display Case Story of the Army Exhibition. National Army Museum. Crown.
Canoeing on the Caldon Canal. Caldon Canal Society.
Regent's Canal, City of Westminster. Inland Waterways Association.
Lions at Blair Drummond, Scotland. Blair Drummond Safari Park.
Sutton Hill, Woodlands Camping Site, Dorset. Camping Club of Great Britain and Ireland. Civi Trust Award 1968. Henk Snoek.
Camping Site, Fermanagh, Castle Archdale, Northern Ireland. NI Tourist Board.
Cockpit at St Fagan's Museum, Cardiff, Wales. National Museum of Wales.
Miniature Railway, Shane's Castle, Northern Ireland. Lord O'Neill.
Gipsy Caravan at St Fagan's Museum, Cardiff, Wales. National Museum of Wales.
Fishing on the Grand Union Canal at Marsworth, Hertfordshire. Inland Waterways Assoc.

A back garden in Stratford Grove, Putney. Alan Smith.
Brighton Square, Sussex. Brighton CBC.
Coombe Abbey Country Park, Coventry. Coombe Abbey Country Park.
The Giles, Pittenweem, Fife, before restoration. National Trust for Scotland.
The Giles, Pittenweem, Fife, after restoration. National Trust for Scotland.
The High Street, Southend-on-Sea, after pedestrianisation. Southend CBC.
Restored shop front, High Street. Haddington. Henk Snoek.
Apothecary's shop, North of England Open Air Museum, Beamish, Co. Durham. Beamish Open Ai Museum.
The Rows, Chester. BTA.
Regent's Canal, City of Westminster. Inland Waterways Association.

Visits

Apart from areas already well-known to the Chairman and Members of the Working Party, special visits were made to the following places:

In England

BERKSHIRE Newbury, Reading
DURHAM Peterlee New Town, Sherburn Hill, Thornley, Byker
ESSEX Southend-on-Sea
HAMPSHIRE Basingstoke
HERTFORDSHIRE Stevenage New Town, Hatfield
KENT Faversham, Tenterden and Meopham
LANCASHIRE Liverpool, Oldham
LINCOLNSHIRE Stamford
NORFOLK Norwich
NORTHUMBERLAND Newcastle-upon-Tyne
OXFORDSHIRE Oxford, Woodeaton
STAFFORDSHIRE Stoke-on-Trent
SUSSEX Horsham, Midhurst, Singleton and St Leonards-on-Sea
TEESSIDE Stockton, Middlesbrough, Thornaby, Billingham
WARWICKSHIRE Coventry
WILTSHIRE Salisbury
YORKSHIRE Leeds, York, Thirsk

In Scotland

GLASGOW Clydebank
COUNTY OF FIFE Dysart, Kirkcaldy, Lochore Meadows
EAST LOTHIAN Haddington, Cockenzie, Dirleton, Preston, East Linton, North Berwick, Yellowcraig, Gullane

In Wales

SWANSEA
CARDIFF

We are most grateful to those members and officers of Local Authorities and members of Civic or Amenity Societies, who gave their time to talk to us and to show us round.

Thanks from the Chairman

I am deeply grateful to:

ROBERT JACKSON, for giving up several weekends to help me cut and arrange the quotations, and for asking Philip Larkin to write the poem, apart from hi inestimable help over the whole Report.

SIMON JENKINS, for his reliability, prompt and professional writing, and excellen advice.

RONNIE NICOLL, for giving us the benefit of his immense knowledge, for suggestin there should be drawings to start each section of the Report, and for his many goo ideas and constant help.

ALFIE WOOD, for his tremendous good humour, his energy, his attention to detail and for sharing with us his expertise and experience of housing, planning an historic buildings.

ANGELA REYNOLDS, for her enthusiasm, her humanity, her commonsens approach, and for giving so much time to visit canals and caravan sites.

You were ideal members and great fun to work with—Thank you all more than can say.

I do want to thank Peter Walker, Secretary of State for the Environment, for givin me the chance to study this fascinating and rewarding subject.

We are all indebted to:

SIR OVE ARUP for his visionary yet practical approach, and thoughtful comments

LORD CLARK for his expert opinion on architecture and the arts, and for placin the environment within the broader canvas of civilisation.

MR MAX NICHOLSON for sharing with us his world-wide experience of ecologica problems, and for writing a brilliant Epilogue.

LORD SNOWDON for the stunning cover photograph.

MR PHILIP LARKIN for the sensitive poem, which we are honoured he wrot especially for the Report.

MR ROY WORSKETT for the highly original and appropriate drawings which begir each section.

MRS SYBIL JOHNSON of Richmond-upon-Thames who, while helping at a luncheor at the Barnes Old People's Day Club, suddenly invented the title of the Report.

In the Department of the Environment

We would like to thank:

MR MICHAEL DAVIS, Assistant Secretary, for his wisdom and guidance, and his constant interest in our work, despite many other pressing responsibilities.

MR KENNETH EVANS for his kindness and active help, and for his absolute dedication to duty, which made us all proud of the British Civil Service.

MISS KATHERINE RENNIE for doing so much tedious checking and rechecking, with such good humour, and for her reliable help over small details.

MR STEPHEN TAYLOR for accompanying us on many visits, and for dealing with day to day work.

MR JAMES LEWIS who was so helpful over the photographs, until promoted just before Christmas.

MRS CONNOLLY, Library, for coping with the index.

THE GIRLS IN THE TYPING POOL for their endless patience in re-typing the Report.

We want to mention especially:

MR ASHLEY BARKER, Surveyor of Historic Buildings to the Greater London Council for so much technical advice, and for checking the typescript of the section on 'Conservation Areas and Historic Buildings'.

MR MICHAEL MIDDLETON, Director, The Civic Trust, for his great help in so many ways, and for giving up his time to discuss finance and taxation in relation to historic buildings.

MR VIVIAN LIPMAN, Assistant Secretary at the Department of the Environment, who always wants to remain anonymous, but who is the marvellous guardian of our historic heritage in the corridors of power, for his continual help and kindness.

PROFESSOR SIR COLIN BUCHANAN who gave up a whole afternoon to discuss traffic problems of all kinds.

THE DIRECTORS AND STAFF OF IMPERIAL CHEMICAL INDUSTRIES who gave their time to see us in connection with our section on Industry and Commerce.

THE ROYAL INSTITUTE OF BRITISH ARCHITECTS for the interesting discussion when we called on them.

THE ENGLISH TOURIST BOARD who provided much helpful information, and some of the beautiful photographs of different parts of England.

THE CAMPING CLUB OF GREAT BRITAIN AND IRELAND for several suggestions.

THE CARAVAN CLUB OF GREAT BRITAIN AND IRELAND for advice and help.

MR KENNETH BLESSLEY, Valuer to the Greater London Council, for information and advice on compensation.

HL—O

MR JOHN FITZPATRICK, Planning Department, Greater London Council, fo information on the history of the Planning Acts.

DR ROY STRONG, Director, The National Portrait Gallery, for his generous hel over our paragraphs on museums.

MR JAMES THOMAS, Greater London Council Historic Buildings Division, fo information regarding historic buildings.

MR DAVID HALL, Director, Town and Country Planning Association, who gav me the names of several Planning Officers who subsequently sent excellent con tributions.

MR LEADER, of Her Majesty's Stationery Office, for taking so much trouble ove the printing of the Report.

MRS CAROLINE WHITE for designing the excellent layout.

EVERYONE WHO SENT SUCH INTERESTING PHOTOGRAPHS of which we ur fortunately could publish only a limited number.

FINALLY

We thank all those people who sent us contributions, and all those who will rea our Report, and who may, we earnestly hope, find it both useful and constructiv in answering the question 'How do we want to live?'

Bibliography

AUTHOR	TITLE	PUBLISHER
Colin Buchanan & Partners	The Prospect for Housing	Nationwide Building Society 1971
Edited by H R Buchanan Emrys Jones and Desmond McCourt	Man and His Habitat	Routledge and Kegan Paul 1971
Reyner Banham	Los Angeles	Allen Lane Penguin Press 1971
Professor Ronald Nicoll and Sir William Lithgow	Ocean Span Eurospan	Scottish Council for Development and Industry 1970
John Aldridge	In the Country of the Young	Chatto and Windus
Theo Crosby	The Necessary Monument	Studio Vista
Asa Briggs	Victorian Cities	Odhams Press 1963 or new edition Penguin 1968
A M Edwards and G P Wibberley	An Agricultural Land Budget for Britain 1965-2000	Ashford—Wye College 1971
Edited by P H G Hettena and G N Syer	Decade of Decision	The Conservation Society
Rachel Carson	Silent Spring	Hamish Hamilton 1963
Roy Worskett	The Character of Towns	Architectural Press 1963
Max Nicholson	The Environmental Revolution	Hodder and Stoughton 1970
Hermione Hobhouse	Thomas Cubitt	Macmillan 1971
Ben Whitaker and Kenneth Browne	Parks for People	Seeley Service 1971
R E Pahl	Whose City?	Longmans 1970
Margaret Whinney	Wren	Thames and Hudson
Anthony Swaine	Faversham Conserved	Borough of Faversham Kent County Council 1969
Frederick MacManus & Partners	Tenterden Explored	Kent County Council 1967
A A Wood	Conservation in Norwich	Norwich City Council
Nikolaus Pevsner	Pioneers of Modern Design	Penguin Books

AUTHOR	TITLE	PUBLISHER
Ralph Dutton	The English Country House	Batsford 1962
Le Corbusier	The Radiant City	Faber & Faber 1967
	Do You Care About Historic Buildings?	Greater London Council
Kenneth Clark	Civilisation	John Murray 1969
Suffolk Preservation Society	Bury St Edmunds Town Centre Study	East Suffolk County Council Suffolk Preservation Society 1971
H S Goodhard-Rendel	English Architecture since the Regency	Constable 1953
Hugh McKnight	Canal & River Craft	David & Charles
Edited by Edward Goldsmith	Can Britain Survive?	Tom Stacey 1971
Hugh Trevor-Roper	The Rise of Christian Europe	Thames & Hudson
Gerald Burke	Towns in the Making	Edward Arnold 1971
Simon Jenkins	A City at Risk	Hutchinson 1970
Jane Jacobs	The Death and Life of Great American Cities	Jonathan Cape 1962
Professor Page	Biology and the Future of Man	Institution of Civil Engineers
B P Moore	Environmental Improvement and Urban Renewal	Institution of Civil Engineers
Reyner Banham, Peter Hall, Cedric Price	Non Plan, an experiment in Freedom	New Society 1969 Vol 13 March 20
	Explorations into Urban Structure	University of Pennsylvania Press
Christopher Alexander	A City is not a Tree	Design 1966 No 206 Feb pp 46-55
	Deptford—a new look	Lewisham Borough Council
Asa Briggs	The Sense of Place (paper—Smithsonian Annual No 2 1968)	Smithsonian Institute
James Silk Buckingham	National Evils and Practical Remedies 1949	Peter Jackson
	Civil Engineering Problems of the South Wales Valleys	Institution of Civil Engineers
	Welsh Environment Journal	University College Cardiff
	Stevenage Master Plan	Stevenage Development Corporation 1966
	Hendon Beaches	Sunderland Civic Society
	Richmond Study: an approach based on environmental management	Richmond Society 1967

AUTHOR	TITLE	PUBLISHER
	Conservation Areas in Redbridge	Redbridge Borough Council
	Conservation in the Development of Northern Ireland: Conference report	Queens University Belfast and Ministry of Development Northern Ireland 1970
	Recreation and London's Reservoirs	Metropolitan Water Board 1970
	Blackheath Conservation Area	London Borough of Lewisham 1969
Richard Llewelyn-Davies	Town Design Colne Valley: Studies for a Regional Park	Liverpool University Borough of Hillingdon (Colne Valley Working Party 1967)
	Tomorrow's London: a background to the Greater London Development Plan	Greater London Council 1969
	The Human Habitat	Greater London Council 1971
	Thirsk, A Conservation Study	Civic Trust for the North East
	Historic Houses Survey	British Tourist Authority and Countryside Commission 1970
	Cyclists To-day	Cyclists Touring Club
	Tomorrow's Glasgow	University of Strathclyde
Colin Buchanan & Partners	Greenwich and Blackheath Study	Buchanan & Partners 1971
	The Arts Council of GB Report 1969-70	The Arts Council
	Meopham Society Report	Meopham Society
Peter Self	Metropolitan Planning	London School of Economics 1971
Kenneth Browne	West End	Architectural Press
British Waterways Board: Birmingham Canal Navigation Working Party	Birmingham Canal Navigations: a report on the 'remainder' waterways	British Waterways Board 1970
Robert Ardrey	African Genesis	Fontana Library
Charles Darwin	The Origin of Species	
J E McKenzie	Low Cost Homes to Rent or Buy	Robert Hale

AUTHOR	TITLE	PUBLISHER
Paul and Anne Ehrlich	Population, Resources, Environment; issues in human ecology	W H Freeman 1970
	Blueprint for Survival	Ecologist, February 1972
Ministry of Transport	Transport planning; the men for the job; a report to the Minister—by Lady Sharp	HMSO 1970
Ministry of Housing and Local Government: Working Party on Sewage Disposal	Taken for granted. Report of the Working Party. (Chairman Lena Jeger)	HMSO 1970
Ministry of Transport	Traffic in towns: a study of the long-term problems of traffic in urban areas; reports of the Steering Group (Chairman Sir Geoffrey Crowther) and the Working Party (Chairman Colin Buchanan)	HMSO 1963
Commission on the Third London Airport	Report (Chairman Hon Mr Justice Roskill)	HMSO 1971
Department of the Environment: Committee on the Rent Acts	Report. Cmnd 4609 (Chairman H E Francis QC)	HMSO 1971
Countryside Commission	Third Report 1969-70	HMSO 1970
Department of the Environment	The future shape of local government finance Cmnd 4741	HMSO 1971
Ministry of Housing and Local Government	York; a study in conservation; report to the Minister . . . and York City Council by Viscount Esher	HMSO 1968
Ministry of Housing and Local Government	Bath; a study in conservation; report to the Minister . . . Bath City Council by Colin Buchanan & Partners	HMSO 1968
Ministry of Housing and Local Government	Living in a slum: a study of St Mary's Oldham. (Design Bulletin 19)	HMSO 1970
Ministry of Housing and Local Government	Cars in housing 1: Some medium density layouts (Design Bulletin 10)	HMSO 1966 (reprinted 1970)
Ministry of Housing and Local Government	Cars in housing 2: I Dimensions. II Multistorey parking garages.	HMSO 1967 (Metric edition HMSO 1971) (Department of the Environment)

Index

Abercrombie, Sir Patrick, 24
Accidents
  causes, 5
Agricultural Land Budget for Britain,
  1965–2000, 145
Agriculture, 131
  land use, 145
Air pollution, 120, 131
Airports, 4, 18, 19, 23
  land use, 121
  VTOL airports, 101
Alexander, Christopher, 20
Amenity societies, 26, 69
Angling, 141
Architects
  contribution to the environment, 41
Architecture, 35–59
  competitions, 59–60
  public opinion of, 57–8
Areas of outstanding natural beauty,
  144, 175
Army Museum, Chelsea, 153–4
Art galleries, 142, 154
Artificial cities, 20
Arts centres
  redundant churches as, 154–6
Arts Council of Great Britain, 143, 154
Arup, Sir Ove, 3
Associated Portland Cement
  Manufacturers, 121
Association of Municipal Corporations,
  39–40, 65
Association of River Authorities, 145
Automobile Association, 100
Aylsham Association, 63, 99–100

Bailey, Michael, 42
Banham, Reyner, 17, 20
Barker, Paul, 20
Barking, London Borough Council, 37
Barlow, Sir Montague, 24
Basingstoke
  industrial area, 23–4
  sports centre, 149
Bath
  traffic tunnel, 70

Bath, A Study in Conservation, 66, 70
Batsford, Brian, 40
Beamish, Co. Durham
  open-air museum, 161–2
Bethnal Green Museum, 153
Billingham
  leisure centre, 149
Biology and the Future of Man, 142
Blair Drummond Safari Park, 158
Boating and Sailing, 141
Bridges, 24
Bridleways, 143–4
Briggs, Asa, 17–18
British Cycling Bureaux, 144
British Mountaineering Council, 120
British Railways Board, 22, 99, 142
British Steel Corporation, 121–2
British Tourist Authority, 6, 143, 159,
  162
Brockham Green Village Society, 19
Browne, Kenneth, 142
Bruton Trust, 65
Buchanan, Colin, 18, 23, 66, 105
Buckinghamshire County Council
  flexible housing, 57
Buildings
  cleaning, 75–8, 96
Bull Ring Centre, Birmingham, 113
Bungalows, 39
Burton St Leonards Society, 63
Bury St Edmunds
  conservation, 70
Bus-only lanes, 111, 116
Bus services, 100, 103, 111
By-passes, 105–6, 116
  for historic towns, 81

Calder Civic Trust, 5, 19
Caldon Canal, 147, 156
Camden, London Borough of
  community preferences, 29
Camping, 161, 166
  Working Party Report, 161
Camping Club of Gt Britain and
  Ireland, 161
Canals, 142, 145, 156, 166

Capital and Counties Property
 Company Ltd, 41
Car ownership, 103, 142
Car parking
 see Parking
Caravan Club, 159
Caravan Sites Act, 1960, 161
Caravans and caravanning, 143
 159–61, 166
Certificate of Secondary Education
 environmental studies, 179
Chandigarh
 artificial cities, 20
Chedworth Society, 21
Chelmsford Society, 143
Chester, A Study in Conservation, 70
Chichester, A Study in Conservation,
 70
Choice
 in community preferences, 29, 34
Churches
 as historic buildings, grants, 87
 redundant, 87, 154–6
Cirencester
 housing, 52
 planning, 12
Cities and towns
 artificial and natural, 20
Citizenship
 environmental education, 167–182
 participation in planning, 26–30
City at Risk, 41–2, 169
Civic Amenities Act, 1967, 71, 74, 92
Civic Society of St Ives, Hunts, 63
Civic Trust, 30, 34, 92
 heavy lorries report, 63, 80
Civic Trust Awards, 1970, 41
Civic Trust for the North West, 122
Civic Trust for Wales, 6
Civil engineers
 contribution to the environment, 5
Civilization, 37
Clark, (Kenneth Mackenzie), Baron
 Clark of Saltwood, 37
Clydebank, 24
Coastal areas
 industry, 138
Cockaigne Housing Association Ltd.,
 42, 52
Cockenzie
 electric power station, 59
Colchester Civic Society, 170
Colin Buchanan & Partners
 Bath study, 66

Commerce, 118–136
Commercial vehicles
 parking, 100
Commission on the Third London
 Airport, 19, 23
 Report, 18
Community centres, 142
Commuting
 transport, 111, 116
Compensation
 compulsory purchase, 24, 31,
 34
Compulsory Purchase Act, 1965, 31
Concert halls, 142
Conservation, 61–92
 finance, grants, 85–90
 local administration, 96
Conservation Areas, 61–92
Contribution of Dispersal, 43
Coombe Abbey
 country park, 158
Cost benefit analysis, 19
Council for British Archaeology,
 63, 87
Council for Environmental Education,
 170
Council for the Protection of Rural
 England, 17, 39, 65, 142
Country Landowners Association,
 66
Country parks, 141, 158–9, 166
Countryside, 17, 21–2, 121, 147
 recreation, 140–166
Countryside Commission for Scotland,
 170
Countryside in 1970, Report, 144–5, 170
 175, 180
Coventry
 foot streets, 114
 housing improvements, 50
 parks and gardens, 148
 shopping precinct, 24
Coventry City Council, 63
Cowan, Peter, 17
Cowburn, William, 39
Crofters Commission, 18
Crosland, Anthony, 38
Crown Estate Commissioners, 121
Crystal Palace
 sports centre, 152
Cublington, 19
Cycling paths, 144

Dartmouth, Countess of, 67
Davies, Richard Llewelyn
    see Llewelyn-Davies, Richard
Death and Life of Great American
    Cities, The, 20, 43
Death duties
    historic buildings, 90, 96
Delinquency
    effects of environment, 6
Denington, Evelyn, 43
Denman, D R, 17
Department of the Environment, 60
    Camping Working Party, 161
    farm buildings control, 138
    films, 30, 34, 180, 181–2
    grants and subsidies, 38
    historic buildings grants, 85, 92
    Long Term Population Trends in Gt
        Britain, 12
    pedestrians, views on, 113
Derelict land
    reclamation, 39, 46, 121–2, 130,
        138, 159, 166
Devonshire
    bungalow development, 39
Disabled persons
    sports facilities, 149
Do You Care About Historic Buildings?
    67
Dutton, Ralph, 141
Dysart
    historic houses restoration, 89

East Anglian Museum of Rural Life,
    Stowmarket, 162
East Hampshire Area of Outstanding
    Natural Beauty, 175
East Neuk of Fife
    historic buildings restoration, 66, 89
Edinburgh
    Meadowbank centre, 152
Edinburgh, HRH the Duke of, 3, 119
Education
    environmental, 167–182
    planning publicity, 29–30, 34
Edwards, A M, 145
Electric power stations
    land use, 121
    siting, 59, 120
Electricity, 138
    overhead supply lines, 131
Elephant and Castle, London
    traffic scheme, 113
Energy and power, 131–4

English Country House, The, 141
Environmental education, 167–182
    planning publicity, 29–30, 34
European Conservation Year, 1970, 180
Expanded towns, 12, 23–4

Farm buildings, 121, 131, 138, 170
Faversham Conserved, 70
Fawkes, Diana, 144
Fife, 24
Films
    in environmental education, 30,
        34, 38, 180, 181–2
Foot streets, 81, 101, 113–4, 116
Footpaths, 143–4
Forestry Commission
    recreational facilities, 144
Forth Road Bridge, 24
Freeman, Hugh, 37–8
Friends of the Lake District, 143, 159

Gardens
    small open spaces, 148
Gardiner, Stephen, 41
Geddes, Sir Patrick, 24
Geffrye Museum, 153
General Certificate of Education
    environmental studies, 179
Georgian Group, 4, 21–2
Glasgow
    foot streets, 114
    parks and walkways, 148
Golborne Neighbourhood Council, 27
Golding, Henry, 63
Goyt Valley
    minibus scheme, 103
Gravel
    land use, 121
    mineral working, 130
Greater London Council, 6, 99
    Historic Buildings Board, 81
Green Belt, London and Home
    Counties Act, 1938, 24
Green Belts, 12, 21, 24
Gregory, Terence, 169

Hackney
    conservation and improvement, 70
    housing improvement, 50
Haddington
    conservation, 71
    leisure centres, 156
    redevelopment, 9

Hall, Peter, 20
Hammerson Group of Companies, 21, 39
Hampshire
  open spaces, 144
Hampshire County Council, 175
Harris, Peter, 100
Harrow
  conservation, 71
Haslemere Estates Ltd, 64
Hatfield
  housing association housing, 52
Hedgerows
  removal, 121, 131
Hettena, Trish, 37
High Wycombe Society, 19
Highfield, M H, 5
Highways Act, 1959, 31
Hillingdon London Borough Council, 19
Historic buildings, 61–92
  cleaning, 75–8, 96
  conservation, 18
  Crown ownership, 87
  destruction, 12, 17
  finance, grants, 85–90
  present day use, 87, 156
Historic Buildings Board
  see Greater London Council
Historic Buildings Council, 66, 85, 89, 92
Historic Buildings Trusts, 89
Historic towns
  by-passes for, 81
Home ownership, 39
Homes Before Roads Campaign, 27
Horncastle Civic Society, 169
Horsham Society, 121
Hounslow London Borough Council, 4
Housing, 35–59
  bungalows, 39
  cost yardstick, 41
  density, 24, 43, 53
    low rise high density, 42
  design preferences, 40, 41, 42
  flexible, 42, 56–7, 60
  improvement, 38, 50, 60, 70, 85–87
  Industrial Revolution, 23
  landscaping, 41, 56, 60
  maintenance, 56
  old people's flats, 75
  public opinion, 45
  residents associations, 27
  social needs and facilities, 38, 53, 60

standards, 46
terraces, 42
Housing associations, 52, 65
Housing, Town Planning Act, 1909, 24
Huddersfield Building Society
  flexible housing competition, 57
Human Zoo, The, 39
Hurley Preservation Society, 21
Hydro-electric power stations, 120

Ilkley Civic Society, 100
Imperial Chemical Industries, 3
Indoor recreation, 142–3
Industrial Management, 1971, 3
Industrial Revolution, 23, 122
Industry, 118–136
  contribution to the environment, 14
  location, 24, 125–7, 129–30
  pollution, 119–20, 125
Information centres
  environmental education, 179–80, 182
  for foreign tourists, 162
Inland waters and waterways, 142, 145, 166
Inland Waterways Association, 145
Innovation
  changing patterns of society, 3–4
Institute of Directors, 121
Institute of Housing Managers, 144
Institution of Civil Engineers, 5
Iron and steel industry
  derelict land, 121–2
Islington
  housing improvement, 50
Islington London Borough Council, 42
Islington Society, 38

Jacobs, Jane, 20, 43
Jenkins, Simon, 41–2, 169
Jones, D, 38
Jones, Emrys, 3–4, 22

Keep Britain Tidy Group, 7
Kings Lynn Preservation Trust, 89
Knutsford Society, 18
Kyoto
  'natural' cities, 20

Lamp of Lothian Collegiate Trust, 156
Land reclamation, 13, 46, 121–2, 130, 139, 159, 166
Land use, 12, 13, 21–2, 46
  airports, 121

electric power stations, 121
gravel working, 121
oil refineries, 121
railways, 22, 39, 46
recreation, 142, 145
sea-gas terminals, 121
zoning, 45
Landscaping
camping sites, 161
housing, 41, 56, 60
iron and steel industry, 122
mineral workings, 130
Le Corbusier, 43
Leeds
express bus service, 111
foot streets, 81
minibus service, 111
Leicester
Clarendon Park improvement area,
27
Leighton Buzzard and District
Preservation Society, 21
Leisure and sports centres, 149–52, 166
Levittown
artificial cities, 20
Lewes
conservation, 18
Lichfield Civic Society, 37, 169
Lithgow, Sir William, 37
Litter, 7, 21
Liverpool
housing improvement, 50
Knowsley Park, 158
natural cities, 20
old people's flats, 75
Llewelyn-Davies, Richard, *Baron
Llewelyn-Davies of Hastoe*, 17
*Local Authorities Historic Buildings
Act, 1962*, 87
Local government
environmental improvement and
conservation committees, 81–5,
64, 96
historic buildings responsibility, 85,
96
local planning committees,
membership, 30, 34
London Motorway Box, 99
*Long Term Population Trends for Gt
Britain*, 12
Loop roads, 106, 110, 116
Lorries
damage to historic buildings, 63, 80
parking, 100

Los Angeles, 17
Ludlow
traffic problem, 80

McLeish, Gordon, 18
Man and His Habitat, 3–4, 22
Manhattan
natural cities, 20
Margate Civic Society, 65
Marylebone Goods Yard, 46
Mason, Peter, 4, 100–101
Merton London Borough Council, 64
Metropolitan Public Gardens
Association, 148
Metropolitan Water Board, 145
Middlesbrough
foot streets, 114
housing improvement, 50
Midhurst Society, 64
Mineral working, 121, 130
Minibus services, 100, 103, 111
Ministry of Housing and Local
Government
flexible housing research, 57
Preservation Policy Group, 90
Skeffington Report, 26
Moore, B P, 20
Morris, Desmond, 39
Motorways
urban, 99–100, 105
Moving pavements, 100
Multi-level traffic ways, 100, 113
Museums, 142, 153–4, 166
open-air, 161–2

National Building Agency
flexible housing, 57
National Buildings Conservation Fund
proposal for, 89, 96
National Council of Women of Gt
Britain, 121
National Farmers Union, 138, 144
National Federation of Housing
Societies, 52, 65
National House Builders Registration
Council, 40
National Information Centre
proposal for, 180, 182
National parks, 158
National Trust, 89, 144, 158
National Trust for Scotland, 66, 89
National Union of Journalists, 5
National Union of Townswomen's
Guilds, 4

Natural cities, 20
Nature trails, 159, 166
Neighbourhood councils, 27
New towns, 20, 24
Newbury
  relief road, 80
Nicoll, Ronald, 37
Northern Ireland
  conservation, 66
North-west England
  economy, 122
Norwich
  foot streets, 81, 113
  housing improvement, 50
  road system, 106
Norwich City Council, 101
Norwood Society, 21
Nuclear power, 131–4
  power station land use, 121

Oceanspan, 37
Offices, 127, 138
Oil refineries
  land use, 121
Outdoor recreation, 140–164

Page, J K, 120, 142
Pahl, R E, 18–19, 99
Parker-Morris standards, 46
Parking, 99–100, 107–10, 116
Parks, 158–9, 166
  country, 141
  National, 158
  town, 142, 147–8
  wildlife, 158
Pedestrians, 111–114
  foot streets, 81, 99, 101, 113–4, 116
Pedestrians Association for Road
  Safety, 99
Pershore Civic Society, 21, 38
Petersfield Society, 141
Pevsner, Sir Nikolaus, 41
Pinner High Street
  conservation, 71
Pioneers of Modern Design, 41
Pipelines
  underground, 134
Planning
  achievements, 17, 23
  administration, 21, 31–2
  cost benefit analysis, 19
  development control, 22
  fashions in, 20
  history, origins, 23

law, 17, 24, 27, 45, 92
local planning committees,
  membership, 30, 34
professions, 4, 18–19, 23, 24, 32
  171, 175–6
public participation, 19, 26–30
publicity, exhibitions, 29–30, 34
social needs, 9, 18, 19, 20, 22
strategic planning, 24, 27
Plymouth
  city centre, 6
Plymouth Barbican Trust, 89
Plymouth Humanist Group, 5
Pollution
  air, 120, 131
  industrial, 119–20, 125
  Royal Commission, 119
Population, 12
  urban, 45, 52, 60, 141
Porter, Sir George, 119
Preservation Policy Group
  Report, 90
Press
  Admission to planning committee
    meetings, 30, 34
Price, Cedric, 20
Private bus operators
  licensing, 111, 116
Public transport, 100, 110–11
  116, 142
Putney
  conservation, 64

Quality of life and environment, 3, 4,
  134, 138

Race courses
  as camping sites, 161
Railways, 99, 142
  disused, 142, 148
  land use, 22, 39, 46
Ramblers Association, 121, 143–4
Rateable value
  housing improvement, 50, 60
Rayleigh Civic Society, 63
Recreation, 140–164
  land use, 142, 145
Redundant Churches Fund, 87
Regents Canal, 156
Reilly, Sir Paul, 6
Reynolds, Angela, 64
Richmond Society, Surrey, 99
Richmond-upon-Thames
  traffic plan, 27

Rights of way, 143–4, 164
Ring roads, 24, 106, 116
Rivers, 145
  walkways, 156, 167
Road Research Laboratory, 107
Roads, 98–115
Roberts, Hugh, 4–5
Roskill Commission
    see Commission on the Third
    London Airport
Royal Commission on Environmental
    Pollution, 119
Royal Institute of British Architects,
    41
  flexible housing competition, 57
Royal Institution of Chartered
    Surveyors, 4, 40
Royal Society for the Prevention of
    Accidents, 5
Royal Society for the Protection of
    Birds, 6–7
Royal Society of Arts, 119–20
Royal Society of Health, 39
Rural studies
    see Environmental education

Sailing
    see Boating and sailing
St Agnes Amenity Society, 141
St Fagans
  Welsh Folk Museum, 161
St Fagan's Village Association, 63
St Ives, (Hunts) Civic Society, 63
St Katherine Dock, London
    Redevelopment, 46
Salisbury
  shopping precinct, 75
  town centre development cost, 21
Sandys, Duncan, 71
Schools, 53
Science and the City, 17
Scott, Lord Justice, 24
Scottish Landowners Federation, 121
Sea gas terminals
  land use, 121
Sense of Place, The, 17–18
Sharp (Evelyn), Baroness Sharp of
    Hornsey, 171, 175, 176
Sheffield County Borough Council, 20
Shepherd, Peter, 40
Shopping facilities, 53, 127–9
  out of town, 105, 129, 138
  parking, 99–100
  precincts, 24, 75, 114

Siena
  natural cities, 20
Singleton, Sussex
  open-air museum, 161
Skeffington Report, 1969, 26
Social and Community Planning
    Research
  community preferences, 29
Society for the Protection of Ancient
    Buildings, 4, 21–2
South East England
  population, 13
  strategy plan, 13
South Wales and Monmouthshire
    Housing Association, 52
Southend-on-Sea
  foot streets, 114
Sport
    see Recreation
Sports centres
    see Leisure and sports centres
Stafford Historical and Civic Society,
    143
Stevenage
  new town, 23
  landscaping, 56
Stockton-on-Tees
  Preston Hall Museum, 153
Stone cleaning, 75–8, 96
Strategic Plan for the South-East, 13
Strategic planning, 13, 24, 27
Street Defence Leagues, 27
Street furniture
  in conservation areas, 71, 75
Strong, Roy, 154
Structure plans, 24
Study in Countryside Conservation,
    175
Suffolk Preservation Society, 70

Taken for Granted, 141
Tax rebates
  repairs to historic buildings, 90, 96
Tay Road Bridge, 24
Taylor Woodrow Property Company
    170
Teachers
  training in environmental education,
    170, 176, 181
Television
  in environmental education,
    38, 182

Tenterden
  traffic problem, 80
Terrace housing, 42
Tewkesbury
  effects of M5 motorway, 81
Theatres, 142–3
Theatrical Management Association,
  143
Third London Airport, 4, 18, 19, 23
Thirsk
  traffic problem, 80
Thompson, T A, 3
Thornaby-on-Tees
  leisure centre, 152
  town centre, 24
Toll roads, 107
Tomorrow's Glasgow, 142
Tomorrow's London, 6
Tourist industry, 6, 143, 162
Towards a Labour Housing Policy, 1971,
  38
Tower Hamlets
  redevelopment, 46
Town and Country Planning Act, 1947,
  24, 45, 58
Town and Country Planning Act, 1968,
  24, 27, 69, 92
Town and Country Planning Act, 1969,
  24, 27
Town and Country Planning
  Association, 30, 34
Town centres
  depopulation, 45, 52
Town Development Act, 1952, 23–4
Traffic, 98–115
  conservation areas, 80–81
  management, 27, 106–7, 116
Traffic in Towns, 105
Transport, 98–115
  planning profession, 171, 176
*Transport Planning; The Men for the
  Job*, 171, 176
Travel modes
  preferences, 142

Ulster Architectural Heritage Society, 2
Ulster Farmers Union, 144
Underground facilities, 100
Underground pipelines, 134, 138
Urban District Councils Association, 6
Urban motorways, 99, 100, 105
Urban renewal
  general improvement areas, 27
Uthwatt, Augustus Andrewes, *Baron
  Uthwatt of Lathbury*, 24

Vandalism, 19
Victoria and Albert Museum, 154
Victorian Society, 4, 21–2, 42
Villages
  within cities, 6

Wandsworth London Borough Council
  66
Wanstead Residents Society, 5
Water sports, 141
Water supply, 145
Weald of Kent Preservation Society,
  65, 170–1
Weddle, A E, 120
Welsh Glass Works, Swansea, 59
Westminster Society, 19
Weymouth Civic Society, 65
Whitaker, Ben, 142
Whose City? 18–19, 99
Wibberley, G P, 145
Wiggins, David, 142
Wildlife parks, 158
William Blake House, Soho, 52
Wood, Alfred, 101
Woodley and Earley Society, 142
Worcester
  historic buildings destruction, 17

Yellowcraig, East Lothian
  caravan site, 159
York
  Castle Museum, 153
York, A Study in Conservation, 70
York Civic Trust, 70

Printed in England for Her Majesty's Stationery
Office by McCorquodale Printers Ltd., London
HM 4780 Dd 163160 K30 7/72